WHAT'S A PASTOR TO DO?

THE

GOOD

AND

DIFFICULT

WORK

OF

MINISTRY

D0970665

WHAT'S A PASTOR TO DO?

THE GOOD AND DIFFICULT WORK OF MINISTRY

JEREN ROWELL

Beacon Hill Press of Kansas City
Kansas City, Missouri

Library of Congress Cataloging-in-Publication Data
Rowell, Jeren, 1961-
    What's a pastor to do? : the good and difficult work of ministry / Jeren Rowell.
        p. cm.
    ISBN 0-8341-2207-3 (pbk.)
    1. Pastoral theology—Church of the Nazarene. I. Title.

    BX8699 .N35R69 2004
    253—dc22

                                                                    2004018990

10   9   8   7   6   5   4   3   2   1

DEDICATION

In loving memory of my father, Jimmie Leon Rowell.
As a dedicated layman he loved pastors in word, deed,
and attitude. May his tribe increase!

CONTENTS

Acknowledgments 9

Pastoral Health: Cruel Oxymoron? 11

Pastoral Identity

1. Are You Called or Driven? 13
2. What's a Pastor to Do? 17
3. Quiet Service 19
4. Nurturing the Call 21
5. Getting a Pastor 23
6. The Covenant of Pastor and People 25
7. Good-Faith Leadership 29
8. Careful—Your Leadership Is Showing 31
9. Ministerial Malpractice 33
10. Becoming a "Real" Pastor 35
11. Don't Look Back 37

Pastoral Health

12. Most Dangerous Job 39
13. Tired Pastors 41
14. The High Cost of Obedience 43
15. When You Feel Overwhelmed 45
16. Anger in the Pastor's Study 47
17. Faithful Doubters 49
18. Can a Pastor Keep the Sabbath? 51
19. The Pastor's Private Life 53
20. When Someone Throws Dirt on Your Head 55
21. When Congregations Abuse Pastors 57
22. Failure 59
23. When It's Time to Leave 61

The Pastor as Prophet

24. Are You a Pesky Prophet?   63
25. We Are Christian   65
26. Does Anybody Really Know What Time It Is?   67
27. What to Do About Ornery People   69
28. The Information/Action Ratio   71

The Pastor as Priest

29. Let Us Worship God   73
30. This Is the Word of the Lord   75
31. Worship at the Table   77
32. The Gift of Pastoral Blessing   79
33. Bear the Names   81
34. Let the Children Come   83

The Pastor as Shepherd-King

35. The Pastoral Art of Shaping Worldview   85
36. Pastoral Visitation   87
37. What I Learned While Waiting to Eat BBQ   89
38. 10 Traits of Effective Leaders   91
39. Sexual Healing   93

Notes   95

About the Author   96

ACKNOWLEDGMENTS

I've often heard pastors say something like "I don't think I've ever had an original thought. I'm the master of borrowing and adapting." Most pastors can identify with this to some degree. The scope of our work is so broad that we must rely on helpers along the way.

My pastoral life has been blessed with some of the finest helpers. Ed Wallace was my pastor when I first heard God's call on my life to preach. His nurture and support in those critical early years was inspirational. Richard Young taught me more of the practical side of pastoral ministry than anyone else. I feel indebted to him nearly every day. Eugene Peterson, William Willimon, Thomas Oden, David Hansen, Henri Nouwen, Frederick Buechner, and so many others have shaped my life through their writings. I know that many of their thoughts echo in what I think, say, and write.

Special friends have shared the pastoral office with me over the years, and much of what I *think* I may understand about the work is due to their influence. David Busic, Mark Hayse, and Jeff Hooven deserve specific acknowledgement (or blame!) among this group.

I am grateful for the good people of four Nazarene congregations who loved me through my mistakes and found a way to offer encouragement even when there was little to encourage. My special esteem goes to the people of the Nazarene congregation in Shawnee, Kansas, who have loved me well for the past 13 years.

Like most pastors, I would not have survived even this long without the faithful sustenance of my wife and family. Starla and my children have joined me on this journey in every way, and I am grateful.

Finally, my humble thanks goes to the good people of Beacon Hill Press who have encouraged and helped this work to see the light of day. And to Bob Brower and Kelly Gallagher, who seven years ago gave me the venue to talk to pastors through *The Communicator*, thank you!

Most of the material to follow first appeared in a monthly

newsletter for pastors and church leaders called *The Communicator.* It is a resource review tool from Nazarene Publishing House in Kansas City. In 1998 the leaders of NPH invited me to have a conversation with my pastoral colleagues around the country on the front page. It has been a wonderful journey, and I am glad for everyone who has written over the years with affirmation or criticism. I'm a better pastor because of it!

PASTORAL HEALTH: CRUEL OXYMORON?

"Jesus told this simple story, but they had no idea what he was talking about. So he tried again" (John 10:6, TM).

It's not looking too good for pastors. We're about to join the list of endangered species in North America. Maybe it has something to do with the observation of John in his Gospel, quoted above. Jesus tried and tried to help his followers "get it." Likewise, being a pastor is much about "trying again" to help people grasp the gospel. This is hard work. It is dangerous work. We are trying to call people to become, by God's grace, something that they are not and cannot be on their own. We are indeed trying to call out a world that does not exist. The lofty ideals of the gospel of Jesus Christ often don't make sense to the good, pagan folks we are trying to impact. Borrowing the Parable of the Sower (Mark 4) and applying it to us (instead of to God, which was Jesus' point), we scatter a lot of seed, and some of it falls into good soil. It can be a bit disheartening, however, to realize just how much of the seed falls onto the hardened path and gets eaten up by the pesky birds who have no concern for our hard work.

Much of what we do as pastors falls on hard soil, deaf ears, stubborn hearts, and even dense minds. But we try again. And again. And still again. It's enough to make lesser souls give up in frustration and quit. We, however, keep pressing forward, believing that when all appears lost, grace will burst through and life will emerge where only death would have been expected. This is pastoral life. It's good work. And it's very difficult work.

To embrace pastoral ministry as a life of sacrifice is not a surprise for most of us. We expected sacrifice. What we may not have been totally prepared for, however, was the immense challenge of staying healthy while doing the work. In fact, many pastors do not keep their health. The relentless pressure of pastoral life takes a colossal toll on our spirits, minds, and bodies. Too many of us, without fully realizing it, get into starved conditions spiritually.

We gradually pull away from true relationships (often in response to the pain of relationships) and find ourselves isolated and alone. A majority of us probably fail to take proper care of our bodies. Many pay a big price after years of neglect. As I said to start, *it's not looking too good for us*. According to Kenneth Crow, the average tenure for Nazarene pastors in a congregation now hovers somewhere just over 3 years.[1] Studies also show that a growing number of pastors are out totally after only 15 years in the ministry.

In the face of such realities, is it nothing but a cruel oxymoron to talk about *pastoral health*? While *pastor* and *healthy* may seem incongruous, the truth is that some pastors are able to enjoy a lifetime of productive ministry and emerge healthy—even happy! How do they do it? I am convinced that the foundation of pastoral health is a thoroughly biblical pastoral theology. We get into trouble when we take our cues from the world. While secular systems of business and management have much to teach us, they cannot alone bear the weight of a pastoral calling.

It is from this conviction that the following reflections on pastoral life materialize. I would encourage you to use this book "devotionally." That is, you might want to read one reflection each day as a way to open a space in which the Spirit can speak to you over time about your pastoral health. I pray that in some small way these thoughts might be become a tool in God's hand to strengthen and encourage you. Take care of yourself, Pastor. We need you too badly to lose you too soon.

Pastoral Identity

ARE YOU CALLED OR DRIVEN?

"Early in the morning, Jesus went off to a solitary place, where he prayed. When [the disciples] found him, they exclaimed: 'Everyone is looking for you!' Jesus replied, 'Let us go somewhere else'" (Mark 1:35-38).

I was en route to my first congregational assignment when the question hit me like a ton of bricks: *What have I gotten myself into?* There were many things I did not know. There was one thing, however, for which I was especially ill prepared. How would I deal with the wide variety of expectations that the people in my congregation would have for their pastor?

One of the things I really wanted to know as I began my charge (at least I *thought* I wanted to know it) was *What do these people really need from me?* So (and this is where my naiveté showed up) I asked them!

I'd meet someone in the church and they would say to me, "Oh, we are so glad that you've come to be our pastor."

I'd say, "I'm so glad too. I hope we have a wonderful time together. Please tell me, what do you need from your pastor?"

"Well, that's easy. We need our pastor to be a preacher of the Word, to rightly divide the word of truth. Give us spiritual food that will nourish our lives in Christ. We want you to spend adequate time in study and reflection so that when you step into that pulpit on Sunday it will be obvious that you've been with God and into his Word."

I thought, *Well, OK. I like the sound of that. I can do that.* And I went on my merry way thinking, *This is going to be fun.*

Then I met another person, and that person said to me, "Oh, we are so glad that you've come to be our pastor."

I said, "I'm so glad too. I hope we have a wonderful time together. Please tell me, what do you need from your pastor?"

"Well, that's easy. We need our pastor more than anything to love us and care for us. Please get to know us and spend time with us. We need you to be available to visit us and to know what's happening in our lives. You can be the greatest preacher in the world, but if you aren't a loving shepherd to us, it really won't make much difference."

I thought, *OK. I need to be a good preacher, but I also need to spend a lot of time with the people. That sounds like a big job, but OK. I think I can do that.* And I went on my merry way thinking, I *hope this is going to be fun.*

Then I met another person, and that person said to me, "Oh, we are so glad that you've come to be our pastor."

I said, "I'm so glad too. I hope you like me." Then I swallowed hard and said, "Uh, what is it that you need from your pastor?"

"Well, that's easy. We need our pastor more than anything to be a strong leader. We want you to be decisive, energetic, and creative. Be a visionary, for you know that without a vision, the people perish. We need you to be organized and on top of things, make the thing run well—you know, budgets paid, buildings up to snuff, staff members happy and productive. A smooth-running ship."

I thought, *Oh. Well, let's see now. I need to be a good preacher, spend time with the people, and be a great manager. Wow!* And I went on my way thinking, *What have I gotten myself into?*

Then I met another person, and that person said to me, "Oh, we are so glad that you've come to be our pastor."

I said, "I was, too." Then I braced myself and said through clenched teeth, "Tell me, what do you need from your pastor?"

"Well, that's easy. We need our pastor to be an evangelist. You know, to be out in the community, meeting people, and leading them to the Lord. To model for us, of course, how we should all be doing the same thing."

I thought, *Now let's see. I need to be a good preacher, a loving pastor, a great administrator, and an effective evangelist. Hmmm. This is beginning to look like a 70- or 80-hour week.*

Then I met another person, and that person said to me, "Oh, we are so glad that you've come to be our pastor."

And I said, "What do *you* want?"

It didn't take very long before I knew I was facing a critical decision: Would I live by what others expected of me, or would there be some other guide? How do you deal with the reality of people's expectations in pastoral ministry?

It was about that time that the above verses from the Gospel of Mark came alive to me in a new way. In his characteristic breathless style of narration, Mark (in the space of only 34 verses) gives us the meteoric rise of Jesus from virtual obscurity to national fame. Jesus was a hero. This nobody carpenter's son from Nazareth had become the hottest ticket in town. You'd think Jesus would be thrilled with the progress. He's only a couple of days into his ministry, and already he has the attention of the whole town. I know if it had been me, I would have felt on top of the world—successful and competent.

Early in the morning Jesus found a quiet place to pray. When the disciples woke, they became anxious because Jesus was nowhere to be found and the people wanted more. Isn't that the point at which we would jump to respond to the needs of the people? We do it all the time.

But listen to this: The disciples said, "Everyone is looking for you." And Jesus said, "Let's go elsewhere." How could he say that? Did it come from frustration with the people? No. Listen to the reason: "So I can preach in the nearby villages also. That is why I have come." Purpose. Mission. Focus. Calling.

As I look at the contrast between how Jesus responded and how I would have responded, I am confronted with the difference between being *called* and being *driven*. Drivenness is the insatiable drive to do more and to be more. It's a drive that is often masked by sacrificial motives, but in reality it comes out of deep feelings of inadequacy.

Jesus was clearly and securely focused on what the Father had asked him to do. He knew his calling. He understood his mission. And that's why, when the crowd was clamoring for his attention, he was able to say, "Let's go another way." It wasn't out of unconcern for the crowd. It was out of a crystal-clear vision of what he had been given to do by the Father.

Do you have a clear and secure understanding of who you are

in Christ and what he has asked you to be and to do? If you do not, you will be deterred by the expectations of people.

The only way to take all that you are as a person, throw it into the mix of a congregation, and expect a pastoral ministry to emerge is if you have a strong pastoral theology. *What is it that God is asking me to be and to do in this place, in this time, and for the sake of these people?* Every decision we make about our work must be placed against that call.

WHAT'S A PASTOR TO DO?

I know it was a radical thing to do, but I went to the Bible. Eugene Peterson, Thomas Oden, and the others would have to wait. I had many counselors at my disposal, but I sensed a need to hear the words of Scripture.

The question was "What am I really supposed to be doing?" It was during a sabbatical when such questions, which always seemed to lurk, suddenly thrust themselves to the forefront of my thinking:

- What is a pastor?
- How does a pastor live and work?
- When does a pastor say *yes*?
- When does a pastor say *no*?

The expectations of a congregation are crushing. It's just a matter of multiplication. We might be able to respond fully to the expectations of one person (although marriage would teach us otherwise), but when you get beyond six people in your congregation, forget it! So what we do must come from somewhere other than the expectations of folks. It must come from somewhere other than our own expectations. Often the demands we make of ourselves are unrealistic.

Gladly, the Bible speaks to this issue. During my sabbatical I went to the obvious texts. I read the pastorals over and over again. I studied the pastoral theology of 2 Corinthians. I noted the pattern of the apostles in Acts. I considered the leadership models of Moses, Ezekiel, Nehemiah, Jesus, and others. As I did this, a clear picture of what a pastoral leader is to do began to emerge.

I simply made lists of indicative and imperative statements as I studied each set of texts. There were pages of notes, but reflection revealed that authentic pastoral work really boils down to a few basic patterns. These themes are repeated so often that there is simply no mistaking their import:

- Pastors are to study and preach the Word.
- Pastors are to pray and take time to listen to God.
- Pastors are to give wise counsel and spiritual direction.
- Pastors are to set an example for the people.

That's about it. Now I suspect that most of us believe those things are essential to our work. Yet how many of us find ourselves getting pushed away from that core work and into the choking confusion of what I've heard Marva Dawn call *administrivia*?[2] Even the list from the official *Manual* of the Church of the Nazarene was a bit depressing. There are thirty-two directives for pastors.[3] The first several match up pretty well to the Bible. The rest of them (the majority) basically say, "Run the church." I am not suggesting that those responsibilities are unimportant or should be ignored. But if I allow my pastoral vocation to be dominated by the issues of program and administration, I have stopped being a pastor. The popular model of leadership that would liken a pastor to a corporate CEO simply doesn't carry the freight when it comes to what the Bible says about the core work of a pastor.

Part of the problem is that our people don't understand what we do. Our product-oriented world doesn't value the "nonproductive" activities of prayer and reflection. But pastors want to be valuable. We want to be esteemed as folks who work hard and earn our salaries, so we easily succumb to the temptation to make a lot of noise "running things."[4]

Our challenge, then, is to take our job descriptions not from the expectations of people or even from a denominational polity alone. We take our cues from the Bible. We give ourselves most of all to the core work that the Scriptures outline for us. This will require discipline and strength. We must be disciplined enough to resist being distracted by the myriad of urgent things coming at us every day. We must be strong enough to keep our ordination vows, even when our people want us to do other things.

QUIET SERVICE

I listened to her talk for only about 10 minutes, but I was deeply moved. More accurately, I was humbled. She was just about 25 years old when I met her. Her name is Irena. She's Russian by birth.

Irena became Christian in Russia at age 16. Soon after, she sensed God calling her to a ministry of evangelism, and she knew that preparation was necessary. Somehow she got acquainted with some folks from Korean Nazarene University and ended up in South Korea studying theology and Bible in the Korean language that she learned just so she could study there.

She spoke to us in impeccable English. In fact, she has some seven languages at her disposal. When I met her she had just enrolled in seminary to study with the purpose of entering into a "closed" country to spread the gospel there.

As I listened to her, I said to myself *of* myself, *You poor excuse for a disciple, you haven't done anything!* She was so humble and unassuming. The amazing realization to me was that she would go about her work, and most of the world would never know about it. She'll go into what we now call a "creative access" country, and we won't hear much from her. She'll just be there quietly serving the Lord, faithfully doing what God has called her to do.

Some time later I was in a management conference for pastors, and the leader was talking about the challenge of motivating people in a volunteer organization. He talked about looking for ways to tie specific, tangible rewards to service done in order to encourage more people to give their precious time and resources. He told us that we could no longer expect people in the church to be involved in ministry without being specific about what they stood to get out of it.

Well, like a real dummy, I raised my hand. I asked, "What about motivating people to serve because it's right and it's what God calls us to do?" The people in that room looked at me like I was from another planet. And do you know what the leader's response was? "Good luck." Maybe he was right.

In the Sermon on the Mount Jesus speaks of "acts of righteousness" and the whole thing centers on motive. Why do you do what you do? Jesus is talking about the kind of service where I just go about my ministry, being obedient to what God has called me to do and using the gifts he has given me with no regard for who notices or who doesn't notice. That's not as easy as it sounds. We are wired to need affirmation. Most of us enjoy recognition and praise. That's not what Jesus warns against here. The issue is, has that need for affirmation and praise taken over and become the motivating factor in my service?

The challenge is to take a look at your own discipleship and ask the hard question: *If the truth really be known, why do I do what I do? Does it matter to me whether or not people notice? If I give my life away and nobody ever knows about it, am I OK with that?*

This is a particularly significant issue for pastors. We do so much of our work "up front." People notice what we do. Yet if we're not careful, we can become dependent upon the affirmation and recognition of people.

I was challenged by Irena to refocus my motive for serving the Lord. If I'm really honest, what motivates me to "give it all" in ministry? Do I live out of the Kingdom value of quiet service? Jesus said, "Be especially careful when you are trying to be good so that you don't make a performance out of it. It might be good theater, but the God who made you won't be applauding" (Matthew 6:1, TM).

NURTURING THE CALL

Recently somebody asked me to share about my call to vocational ministry. It's been awhile since I've rehearsed that story. Now with the perspective of more than 25 years, I noticed a critical component to my call that became a fresh challenge to me.

I began to sense God's call to preach at age 15. I owned and verbalized that call at about age 17. I have mostly viewed those two years as the process of my own response and obedience. Upon reflection, however, I now see that what happened during those two years might not have happened without the intentional and faithful influence of others.

My home church was a critical influence. Those dear people had a very simple approach to life and to church. The people and their ministry were not flashy, but those folks nurtured an atmosphere of obedience to the Lord. It was in that atmosphere that I heard and responded to God's voice.

My parents were obviously key influencers. Mom and Dad never suggested to me that I become a preacher. They only suggested that the very best way to live is in total surrender to the will of God. They cast a vision for my life, not in terms of a particular vocation but in terms of being a person who is soldout to the values and patterns of the kingdom of God. And they had great timing. My mother had a powerful experience when I was very small in which she became convinced that the Lord revealed to her my call to preach. She told me about that experience only after I had fully embraced the call myself. So rather than it becoming a self-fulfilling prophecy, it was a beautiful confirmation of God's plan for my life.

Another very important influence was my pastor. I was terrified at the thought of being a pastor and especially a preacher. I did not think of myself as possessing the gifts and graces for that ministry. By age 17, though I still had apprehension, I was willing to admit that God had indeed given me gifts and graces for pastoral ministry. What changed?

Pastor Wallace, having discovered the emerging call of God on my consciousness, brought me into his vocational life. He made me an insider. He talked to me about the joys and the burdens of pastoring. He took me with him to visit the sick. He put me in charge of the music ministry at our church. He showed me how to lead a congregation in worship. He walked me through the process of writing a sermon. Ed and his wife, Margie, invited me to be a regular guest in their home, where I discovered that pastors' families are mostly normal. They loved me and prayed for me and believed in me even when I acted very much like a self-absorbed adolescent.

When God called at age 15, I was terrified. When he was still calling at age 17, I said yes. I now see that it had everything to do with a faithful pastor intentionally nurturing the call. There is the challenge to me. I recognize my responsibility as a pastor to nurture the call of God in the lives of young people in my congregation. I want to return the favor and the blessing. I want always to be looking for the opportunity to bring emerging preachers into my vocational life and show them that while answering God's call is burdensome, it is also full of joy.

Look carefully around your congregation, your sphere of influence. Do you have some young people who are beginning to sense the call of God on their lives and are frightened by that call? What can you do to help create an atmosphere of obedience and to nurture the call?

GETTING A PASTOR

What do laypeople want in their pastors? That was the question studied by Adair T. Lummis in her report of "Answers from Lay Search Committee Chairs and Regional Judicatory Leaders."[5] The following criteria were identified in the study as desirable character- istics and qualities in a pastor that church boards are looking for:

1. *Demonstrated competence and religious authenticity.*
2. *Good preacher and leader of worship.*
3. *Strong spiritual leader.*
4. *Commitment to parish ministry and ability to maintain bound- aries.* Meaning that lay members generally expect their pas- tor to be primarily devoted to ministry and take minimal time for other pursuits.
5. *Available, approachable, and warm pastor with good "people skills."*
6. *Gender, race, marriage, and sexual orientation of clergy.* Typical- ly, search committees want pastors who are married men with children, under age 40, in good health, with more than a decade of experience in ministry.
7. *Age, experience, and job tenure of the pastor.* Laity often want a young married pastor as a way to draw in young families, but also a pastor with experience. The dramatic increase in older, second-career seminarians, however, has changed the relationship between age and experience.
8. *Consensus builder, lay ministry coach, and responsive leader.*
9. *Entrepreneurial evangelists, innovators, and transformational re- flexive leaders.* This area often presents a disconnect between what churches say they want and what they really want.

Much of the stress in pastor-parish relationships goes to unmet expectations. Congregations expect a pastor who will "meet their needs." Pastors expect congregations that will "follow their lead." So what can we do about these expectations and the disappoint- ment that so often goes with them? We need education. Pastoral candidates need strong education in pastoral theology so that they have a clear sense of what it means to be pastor and to do the work of pastor. Without a solid and biblical pastoral theology, we become nothing more than what Stanley Hauerwas calls "a quivering mass of availability."[6]

Congregations need education. Church boards need education. Pastors can help with this by intentionally and carefully teaching their lay leaders some pastoral theology. "What is a pastor? What is a pastor to do? What does it mean for a pastor and people to live together in covenant?" Denominational leaders can help with this by intentionally and carefully helping church boards to think theologically about the role and office of pastor in their community of faith. Our people have been well trained by a consumer culture to think mostly in terms of whether or not their "needs are being met." This is not a Christian way to think. It would be great if some of our best academicians and practical theologians could develop a curriculum to be used by denominational leaders with local church boards when they are in the process of pastoral search, teaching them to ask the right questions and to offer the right commitments.

Getting the right pastor has to be about more than "filling pulpits" and even about more than trusting God's direction, important as that is. We need to be educating our church on the true nature of the covenant between pastor and people (described in the next chapter). Perhaps then the "profile" of pastor will be drawn not so much from culture as from the Bible and from the historic Christian faith.

THE COVENANT OF PASTOR AND PEOPLE

During a sabbatical study I reflected on the following facts. In 1999 the Church of the Nazarene had about 4,500 active pastors in the USA/Canada. Of these pastors, only 270 had served in their assignment more than 15 years. According to data compiled by the Nazarene Research Center, the average pastoral tenure in the Church of the Nazarene is a little more than three years.

It's been widely accepted that long-term pastorates enable the best church growth. However, of these 270 churches that had long-term pastors, 209 were, at the time of the study, in at least a 10-year period of statistical decline. Of course, there have been some great examples of pastors who stayed in one assignment for many years and their congregations experienced great health and growth. But why is it so uncommon in the Church of the Nazarene? Can factors be identified that enable long and healthy tenure with one congregation? These were the questions that drove me to interview a selection of pastors from across the country.

Having researched, interviewed, and reflected on this issue, I came to some tentative conclusions that have only been confirmed in the subsequent years. It is not possible to identify a leadership style, gift set, or personality that enables long pastoral tenure. Individuals with wide diversity of attributes have enjoyed this kind of ministry. It seems that it boils down to one basic factor that is expressed in many different ways. It comes down to a *covenant* that is embraced by pastor and people to live and work together no matter what may come. Outside this kind of covenant, there is no such thing as a *healthy* long-term pastorate.

We learn from the Scriptures that a covenant is a sacred promise made between two parties to live together faithfully through every situation of life whether critical or mundane. This covenant must be remembered, celebrated, and renewed continually in order to give shape to the relationship between its makers. It seems there are two basic reasons this kind of covenant is not commonplace.

First, pastors have a lust for prestige. There is a sick connection between size of congregation and pastoral esteem. I have deep appreciation for the increasing number of leaders who are learning how to celebrate quality as well as quantity.

Second, pastors are smart enough to get out before they are thrown out. Congregations have developed a "disposable" mentality when it comes to pastoral leadership. They think, *If this particular pastoral arrangement doesn't suit us, no problem, we'll just get another one.* It is interesting that an attitude worthy of condemnation in the context of the marriage relationship is embraced in the pastoral relationship. Surely there are differences, but how many "rough spots" could have been overcome if there were more of this kind of commitment?

The only way these sins will be defeated is if pastors and congregations enter, maintain, and renew a sacred covenant of life together as the community of faith. It is our responsibility as pastors to take the lead in teaching our people about this kind of covenant and inviting them to enter into it with us.

LITURGY OF PASTORAL COVENANT

The Secretary of the Church Board Can Serve as Leader

Leader: Pastor, we, your people, charge you to remember your ordination vows.

Congregation: **Preach the Word, be prepared in season and out of season; correct, rebuke and encourage with great patience and careful instruction. Endure hardship, do the work of an evangelist, discharge all the duties of your ministry."** (2 Timothy 4:2-5)

Leader: Pastor, will you affirm this vow and accept again our invitation to be the spiritual leader of this flock?

Pastor: I will.

Leader: Will you, the members of this church, accept, support, and uphold our pastor as he [she] leads us?

Congregation: **We will.**

Leader: Will you affirm your belief that this pastor and this church are to be workers together in the providence of God?

Congregation: **This we do believe and affirm.**

Leader: Will you continue to support this pastor with respect, loyalty, love, and fervent prayer?

Congregation: **This we will do with God's help.**

Leader: Will you continue to receive the pastor's family members as members of our family of faith and love and pray for them as our own?

Congregation: **This we will do with God's help.**

Leader: Will you continue to give sacrificially of your means so that this pastor can be relieved of the temporal cares of this life so that he [she] may give full attention to prayer and the ministry of the Word?

Congregation: **This we will do with God's help.**

Leader: Will you respond to the pastoral leadership by vigorous participation in the congregational life of this church as it carries out its mission of worship, evangelism, nurture, and service?

Congregation: **This we will do with God's help.**

Pastor: In response to the gracious call of God, and in gratitude for the confidence you have expressed in me, I covenant with you to continue living together as an authentic expression of the kingdom of God in this world. I promise
- to lead you in worship, that in our unselfish focus on God we might be shaped in the image of Christ Jesus and truly become His Body;
- to spend time listening to the voice of God, believing that only in hearing Him will I have anything of importance to say to you;
- to preach the Word with boldness and grace, unafraid to be the mouthpiece of the Lord in this place and among these people;

- to study the Scriptures and the teachings of Christ's followers through the ages, that we might be a community of faith rooted in the truth of God and in the historic Christian faith;
- to intercede for you, spending the necessary time to lift you to the throne of God's grace that you might "be built up until we all reach unity in the faith and in the knowledge of the Son of God and become mature, attaining to the whole measure of the fullness of Christ" (Ephesians 4:12-13);
- to give you pastoral care and spiritual direction;
- to lead you in becoming a true community where "each part does its work" (Ephesians 4:16);
- to lead you in serving others, taking up our responsibility to our neighborhood and to our whole world;
- to live before you not only as a pastor but also as a spouse and parent who keeps promises and who lives a balanced life under the lordship of Jesus Christ.

Pastor and people read in unison:
- **We will follow the Bible in living together as a community of faith.**
- **We will love each other with sincerity of heart, choosing to live in grace and forgiveness.**
- **We will honor one another above ourselves.**
- **We will not become lazy or apathetic but will keep our spiritual fervor, serving the Lord.**
- **We will be joyful in hope, patient in affliction, faithful in prayer.**
- **We will share with God's people who are in need and will practice hospitality.**
- **We will live in peace and leave revenge in God's hands.**
- **We will overcome evil with good.**

(Based on Romans 12:9-21)

GOOD-FAITH LEADERSHIP

There's a lot of leadership going on in Judges. Some of it is good. Most of it is bad. Remember the story of Abimelech?

Gideon had led Israel in great victory over the Midianites. The Israelites were so thrilled with his leadership that they wanted to make Gideon their ruler. He wisely resisted, saying, "The Lord will rule over you!" (Judges 8:23, NLT). Under Gideon's watchful eye the people enjoyed peace for 40 years, until he died. Gideon was no more than buried before the people forgot the Lord. That's where all the "leadership" of chapter 9 starts.

Abimelech exercises leadership by killing all 70 of his half-brothers, Gideon's sons. He was thus able to lead the nation unfettered. It only took about three years, however, before Gaal exercised leadership by enticing the people of Shechem to revolt against Abimelech. Then Zebul exercised leadership when he heard about the coup and ran to tell Abimelech what was up. Later, as Abimelech was letting the people of Shechem have it for their rebellion and then while sacking the city of Thebez, an unnamed woman exercised leadership by dropping a millstone on Abimelech's head, crushing his skull. Yep, lots of leadership going on. Effective leadership. Abimelech, Gaal, Zebul—each of them able to get others involved in their mission, destructive as it was.

Oh, by the way, one of Gideon's sons did escape from Abimelech's murder. His name was Jotham. In the midst of all this leadership gone haywire, Jotham climbs Mount Gerizim and shouts a prophecy to anyone who will listen. It's about the nature of true leadership. He says that true leaders act "honorably and in good faith." Jotham repeats those criteria three times in his sermon. (Judges 9:7-21, NLT).

I'm wondering if there might be an important difference between effective leadership and good-faith leadership. There is a lot of talk in the Church these days about leadership. Much of it seems to be based on the values of a materialistic and power-hungry culture. We say we want pastors who are "effective leaders." What does that mean? Very often it seems to mean not much more than the ability to get people lined up behind your mission. No matter that the mission often serves the interests of the culture or of the leader more than of the kingdom of God.

You can be an effective leader and not be a godly leader. You can be an effective leader without being honorable or without leading in good-faith. "Effective" simply means the ability to produce a result. It may not necessarily be the right result. Could it be that good-faith leadership might look like failure to the world and even to your denomination? Could it be that good-faith leadership might result in people falling away? Was Jesus an effective leader? By many of our current standards of leadership, the answer would be no. By the standards of honorable and good-faith leadership, the answer is yes.

What kind of leader are you aspiring to be? What kind of leader is God calling you to be? Perhaps Jotham's prophecy is a word for us. It is possible to lead people effectively in the wrong direction. It is not a question of whether or not you can get things done; it is a question of whether or not you can get the *right* things done.

CAREFUL—YOUR LEADERSHIP IS SHOWING

I'm guessing that Nehemiah didn't wake up one day saying, "I think I'll be a leader." It almost never works that way, perhaps especially for those of us who are pastors. We suddenly find ourselves having been plucked out of a normal life by God's call. Now we are faced with the daunting prospect of leading His often stiff-necked people and realizing we have no clue how to do it. So we set out to read the books and attend the seminars, trying desperately to figure it out.

Have you noticed, though, that some people who read all the books and attend all the seminars are still crummy leaders? And there are others who never read the books or go to seminars who become great leaders. What is up with that? I know that in this result-oriented, product-based, consumer-driven culture of ours, I often get tricked into thinking that my leadership has everything to do with what I *do*. Actually I think it has a lot more to do with who I *am*. Thinking about that again drew my attention back to Nehemiah. I like to occasionally reread the Bible stories of great leaders. It helps me to remember that their "success" was not based so much on knowing the right stuff as on being in a place where they heard God speak and were willing to obey. Here are some of the leadership principles that I remember while reading Nehemiah:

A leader will have genuine compassion and love for the people he or she leads—a desire to see them experience God's very best. This is what brought Nehemiah into leadership. He saw the deep of need of his people and was moved by love to do something about it (Nehemiah 1:1-4).

A leader doesn't act before he or she has spent time alone with God in prayer. Nehemiah's first response was a time of mourning, fasting, and prayer before God (Nehemiah 1:4).

A leader is willing and able to overcome fear and take risks for the sake of the vision. Nehemiah was afraid to speak to the king on behalf of his people—but he did (Nehemiah 2:2-3).

A leader knows and accepts the fact that when one attempts anything significant, there will be opposition and negative people to contend with. Nehemiah no sooner finished his presentation to the king than two of the king's officials became critical of it (Nehemiah 2:10).

A leader does his or her homework, studies the situation, evaluates possible solutions, and is careful and timely about communication. Nehemiah scoped out the project before he started talking publicly about it. He timed his communication carefully (Nehemiah 2:11-18).

Throughout the story of Nehemiah, principles like those can be identified. Here are a few more I notice:

- A leader constantly names God's activity in the midst of the people.
- A leader confronts sin and disobedience strongly.
- A leader exercises great caution and integrity with regard to remuneration and privilege.
- A leader is mindful of the personal identities and stories of his or her people.
- A leader keeps the worship of God central in the life of the community.

I'm sure there are other leadership principles that could be gleaned from Nehemiah's life. What impresses me, though, is that apparently at no point did Nehemiah become self-conscious about his leadership. It seems that he wasn't so much trying to be leader as he was simply trying to be faithful to a passionate vision that God had given him to be an agent of restoration among his people.

I want to be a leader like that. I want it not to matter if my work is never recognized by the world or even by the church as being "good leadership." But I want it to matter greatly that my life is marked by a pattern of faithfulness and obedience to a vision that God has given me for the healing and reconciliation of His people. Yes, it's what I do. But more important, it's who I am.

MINISTERIAL MALPRACTICE

My heart broke as I listened to them pour out their painful story. She sobbed almost uncontrollably. He sat stiffly, nearly in a daze. They had been deeply hurt. In fact, I thought to myself as I listened, *These people have been abused.* The most difficult part of it was that their pain was over a broken relationship with their pastor.

All of us who are pastors know that inevitably someone in our congregation will be disappointed with us. We must even admit that in our humanness we sometimes hurt the people we are charged to shepherd. That's not what I'm talking about here. I am referring to a pattern of calculated mistreatment that was inflicted on these people by their pastor. As I reflected on all they had been through, a phrase popped into my mind: "ministerial malpractice."

Physicians and other professionals do their work these days under the threat of malpractice. Failure to deliver a "standard of care" can result in serious consequences. Doctors spend huge amounts of money for malpractice insurance. Patients have come to expect a certain standard from their doctors, and when that standard is grossly ignored or failed, the potential exists for legal reprisal.

I am not an attorney and do not understand the highly technical arena of malpractice litigation. But it seems that some lessons could be taken from what is expected of physicians who have no higher ethical responsibility to their patients than pastors have to their people. I assume that the basic point of malpractice litigation is that a generally accepted standard of care has been breached to such a degree that harm has been done. I am suggesting that a careless pastor can do serious harm to the spiritual wellbeing of his or her people. So what constitutes ministerial malpractice? I think these might qualify:

- Failure to exercise spiritual authority in a manner consistent with the law of perfect love. "Love does no harm to its neighbor" (Romans 13:10).
- Failure to teach people the historic Christian faith and to faithfully administer the sacraments of the Church.

- Failure to defend the people from the lies of false teachers.
- Using people simply to advance the goals of an organization or personal ambition.

There are many other and probably better ways to describe it, but ministerial malpractice consists in abdicating the basic tools of pastoral ministry: fervent prayer, truthful teaching, and wise spiritual direction—each of which is faithful only when done from love. The Apostle Paul in 2 Corinthians mentions several core characteristics of faithful ministry:

- We have conducted ourselves . . . in holiness and sincerity (1:12).
- We do not peddle the word of God for profit (2:17).
- We do not use deception nor do we distort the word of God . . . [we set] forth the truth plainly. We do not preach ourselves (4:2, 5).
- Christ's love compels us (5:14).
- We put no stumbling block in anyone's path (6:3).
- We are not withholding our affection from you (6:12).
- We have wronged no one, we have corrupted no one, we have exploited no one (7:2).
- We are taking pains to do what is right, not only in the eyes of the Lord but also in the eyes of men (8:21).
- I have kept myself from being a burden to you in any way (11:9).
- I will very gladly spend for you everything I have and expend myself as well (12:15).

Pastors have a sacred responsibility in this work to which we have been called. We have been assigned the care of souls—delicate work indeed. It can be done carelessly and abusively, but it can also be done faithfully and skillfully by the grace of God. In your pastoral work, are you delivering a reasonable standard of care to your people with integrity? May the Holy Spirit enable you to serve the people as Jesus would serve them.

BECOMING A "REAL" PASTOR

I spent 12 years of my ministerial career as an associate pastor. The Lord blessed me with colleagues and lead pastors who valued my role as an associate and esteemed me in the congregation. Nevertheless, I still had well-meaning folks occasionally ask me when I was going to become a real pastor or when I was going to get my own church. I'm really not sure that they intended to communicate the message I received. I think they were only trying to affirm the presence of pastoral gifts and graces in my life. But what I heard was "As long as you stay in this role, you're not *really* a pastor."

I instinctively knew better. I knew that the character and quality of my work in those congregations was truly pastoral. I was listening to God, listening to the people, praying for them, and giving them the very best spiritual direction I could, by God's grace. Even though my program responsibility was narrower and more specific than it is now, I still felt much of the pastoral burden and care for the people that I feel now as a lead pastor in a multiple staff.

My senior pastors also helped me to know that I was not in a second-class position. They valued my work in the congregation, trusted me to deliver pastoral care to the people, and refused to relegate me to second-class status in any way.

As a denomination, we are still learning to adjust to the emerging role of those who are not the lead or senior pastor but are pastors no less. Associate pastors are finding an increasingly significant place in professional ministry.

It seems that we are increasingly in need of a philosophy and theology of pastoral ministry that can recognize and embrace the place of all pastors, whether or not they are the primary preachers or administrative leaders of the congregation. Sometimes it's the misinformed perceptions of laypersons that perpetuate this "second-class" mentality, and sometimes it's the nature of our own system that sets this up. I think several things are needed, but here are three ideas:

- Lead pastors need a multiple-staff philosophy that understands "pastor" as an office and not as one person with a particular title. We must help our congregations understand that when any member of the pastoral team has cared for them, the pastor has cared for them. Lead pastors must also work to build to the pastoral esteem of staff members in the congregation. This can be as small as referring to them as "Pastor" and as large as working toward relative equity in staff salaries.

- Associate pastors must embrace a deeper level of ownership for pastoral care and leadership. Most lead "Pastors" carry a deep and perpetual burden for the people in their charge. They are willing to do whatever it takes to care for them and lead them. Associates should have the same passion and commitment. If you want to punch a 9-to-5 clock five days a week and then expect the same esteem as your lead pastor who accepts his or her role as 24/7, you're missing the mark. That doesn't mean that you have to become an unbalanced workaholic to be esteemed, but you must demonstrate an unqualified commitment to the burdensome task of pastoring.

- Denominational structures, including *Manual* sections related to the ministry, publications, composition of district boards, and attitudes of leadership must guard against discrimination toward the associate pastor.

Authentic pastoral ministry is not a matter of place on an organizational chart. Becoming a "real" pastor involves living faithfully in the midst of a people as prophet, priest, and shepherd. It doesn't matter whether the sign on your office says *associate* or *senior* or anything else. Follow the invitation of Jesus with all of your heart, soul, and strength to "Take care of my sheep" (John 21:16) and you are a "real" pastor indeed.

DON'T LOOK BACK

The life to which Christ has called us is tough; it is no walk in the park, nor is it a pleasure cruise. The challenge to follow Jesus is the most demanding and costly kind of life.

In his Gospel version, Luke relates some words of Jesus about measuring carefully the cost that is associated with being a fully devoted disciple (Luke 9:57-62). Jesus makes abundantly clear to his disciples just what this involves. One thing is clear—it's not a partial cost. It's not a percentage. It's everything. In fact, with Jesus, it's all or nothing. That's the radical demand of discipleship.

It's instructive to hear Luke tell about the kind of responses Jesus got to his unqualified call. Three would-be followers reveal their preparedness to follow Jesus. The first man thinks he is ready: "Jesus, I will follow you wherever you go." I don't think he quite got the connection that Jesus was on his way to Jerusalem to give himself up to a cross. So Jesus talks about foxes and birds and the Son of Man having no place to lay his head. Animals at the mercy of nature have more security than one who is about to be crucified.

The second man says he wants to go and bury his father. Sounds like a valid request. Truth is, in that culture death and burial were separated by hours, not days, so his father probably wasn't even dead yet. It was an excuse.

The third man has a reasonable sounding request: "Just let me go say goodbye to my family." What could be so wrong with that? In fact, we'd think ill of him if he didn't want to do that. But Jesus still calls him to a different priority. There are a lot of good choices in life—a lot of noble things to which you can give yourself—but the call of Jesus is for reckless abandonment to the way of the Cross.

That's the standard of discipleship that Jesus has clearly set. Yet we so often try to soft-pedal the demands of the gospel. We serve a people who regularly tempt us to make the gospel nonintrusive to their materialistic lives.

Eugene Peterson writes, "Religion in our time has been captured by the tourist mindset. Christians have adopted the lifestyle of a tourist and only want the high points."[7] No wonder Jesus spoke so emphatically. This is a hard saying, but there it is confronting us and calling us to more. Jesus said, "No one who puts his hand to the plow and looks back is fit for service in the kingdom of God" (Luke 9:62). Jesus calls us to a life of looking ahead and not looking back. What exactly does that mean? Allow me to suggest some things.

First, it requires a life no longer defined by the past. I don't have to tell you, Pastor, just how "spiritually stuck" some folks can become. It can happen to us too. The problem is not in the power of God to change our lives. The problem is our unwillingness to let go of life as it is and look forward instead of backward.

Jesus makes it clear that forward-looking discipleship requires letting go of our need for self-security. It also includes family priorities that are set straight. In American Christian culture we have made an idol of the nuclear family. Understand—how I treat my family *is* a major part of my discipleship, but God will never call me to place family relationships above total abandonment to His will. That's a scandalous idea, and many Christians refuse to believe it.

But according to Jesus, those are the kinds of issues that will absolutely have to be settled before we can know the deepest levels of genuine discipleship. I am being called to let go of what is. I am being called to keep my eyes focused on Jesus. I can't look back.

It's the attitude and commitment expressed in the prayer of John Wesley:

> *I am no longer my own, but Thine.*
> *Put me to what Thou wilt, rank me with whom Thou wilt.*
> *Put me to doing, put me to suffering.*
> *Let me be employed by Thee or laid aside for Thee,*
> *Exalted for Thee or brought low by Thee.*
> *Let me be full, let me be empty.*
> *Let me have all things, let me have nothing.*[8]

As pastors, the call of Jesus to us is exacting and costly. It's also worth everything. It's worth far more than anything this world has ever offered to us. Don't look back.

Pastoral Health

MOST DANGEROUS JOB

Try this quiz: What are the top five most dangerous professions? U.S. Department of Labor statistics reveal that these jobs are among the most dangerous of all: *Commercial fisherman, logger, truck driver, miner,* and *firefighter.* I'm glad that I don't do any of those. I resonate with Hawkeye Pierce of *M*A*S*H** fame when he said, "The emblem on my family crest is a cringing chicken." However, I want to know how they overlooked *pastor* in the list of most dangerous jobs. Don't you think being a pastor is a dangerous job? I sure do.

It's dangerous to stand as a representative of Christ before the congregation and dare to proclaim, "Thus says the Lord." It's dangerous to stand in the gap between a holy God and a culture that seems to revel in decadence. It's dangerous to receive the confessions of people whose lives have been wrecked by sin. It's dangerous to be placed on a pedestal by well-meaning parishioners who forget that you are but a jar of clay. Sometimes I feel like Uzzah, who reached out his hand to steady the toppling Ark of the Covenant and got zapped (see 2 Samuel 6). This is dangerous, dangerous work!

I've known it for a long time. It didn't take many years in full-time pastoral ministry to discover the peculiar burdens of the shepherd. Lately, though, I've come to understand the danger a bit differently. A while back a friend got me to read the work of Scottish novelist and preacher George MacDonald. Some of you are no doubt familiar with his work, but what a delightful surprise this was to me! *The Curate's Awakening* is a wonderful story of the spiritual renewal of one who had been "going through the motions" of ministry.

Toward the end of the book, MacDonald makes a profound observation about the danger of being enmeshed in the life of the Church. The words struck me hard: "Nothing is so deadening to the divine as a habitual dealing with the outsides of holy things." Would you please go back and read that over, slowly, a couple of times? I was stopped cold in my reading when those words fell like hammer blows on my consciousness. "Oh, Lord, have I become so *professional* that my spirit is dull to you? Have I spent so much energy with the *'outsides* of holy things' that I risk missing the surprising movements of your grace? Have I in any way begun to believe that I am setting the tempo for the rhythms of the Spirit?"

Uzzah's problem in the Samuel narrative was not that he was trying to do something helpful for God. It's that he (and all of Israel, in fact) forgot he was only an instrument. They thought they could take matters into their own hands and secure the presence of God. Uzzah's problem is also my problem. On a recent Sunday morning I found myself becoming upset, even angry, when the service wasn't going the way that *I* wanted it to go. I should have heard the Lord saying, "Do you really think that I can't work with that?" I was all caught up with the "outsides of holy things," and my spirit was in peril of becoming "deadened to the divine" in that moment.

Pastor, don't ever forget how dangerous is this work. Let's be careful to not become so consumed with managing the *outsides* that we wake up one day to discover a deadness of spirit, a cynicism about the Church that we cannot work through, or even anger toward God that he won't cooperate with our plans. This is a most dangerous job. So please be careful.

TIRED PASTORS

It's 9:30 in the morning, and I'm ready for a nap. I was up at 4:30 today simply because I was awakened with a cacophony of thoughts crashing through my mind about the tasks I must complete today. I know that I am nothing special in this. Every pastor I encounter talks about the overwhelming to-do list that goes with this amazing calling.

Recently I was with a number of colleagues from around my region of the country. Every one of them had stories to share about how *tired* we pastors seem to be all the time. Physician Daniel Spaite speaks of this in his wonderful book, *Time Bomb in the Church: Defusing Pastoral Burnout* (Beacon Hill Press of Kansas City). Dr. Spaite cites Rick Ryding's Ph.D. dissertation in which he documented how pastors evaluated their specific activities. Their average workweek was more than 62 hours, but even more significantly they were able to identify, on average, some 255 separate work activities, each averaging 15 minutes in length. As Dr. Spaite says, "It's no wonder a pastor feels fragmented and overwhelmed." And I don't think this is the whining of a younger generation of pastors. My colleagues with more than 30 years experience in pastoral ministry seem to acknowledge that the vise has tightened significantly as we have moved into the postmodern era.

What has happened? And what can be done about it? Clearly this subject needs much thought, research, and dialogue. In my own experience, however, I resonate with the observations of Will Willimon, who speaks to this problem in his book *Pastor: The Theology and Practice of Ordained Ministry*. Willimon pins the problem on us pastors. We have allowed the world to squeeze us into its mold. We have allowed congregations to squeeze us into their particular molds. We are trying to do this pastoral work in a culture where the supreme value is consuming. In this atmosphere the role of pastor has too often been corrupted from shepherd to cruise director. Willimon says it better than I do:

> One reason many pastors become so exhausted by the demands of ministry is that they enter ministry with little basis

for it other than "meeting people's needs." That is dangerous in a society of omnivorous desire, where people, not knowing which desires are worth fulfilling, merely grab at everything.[9]

I have personally discovered that finding a way out of the exhaustion of pastoral ministry has less to do with managing schedules or delegating work and more to do with being lashed to a pastoral theology that will not allow me to give my life to the purposes of contemporary culture but to the purposes of the kingdom of God. When I do my core work, I am encouraged and strengthened. When I forget my core work, I am tired.

May the Lord help us to remember whom we are and what it is that he has called us to do.

THE HIGH COST
OF OBEDIENCE

Do you remember Cathy Freeman? She's the Australian sprinter who during the summer of 2000 not only won the Olympic gold medal that all of Australia craved but also became the first Aborigine to earn a medal at the Olympics.

Just after her victory an amazing thing happened. As the cameras zoomed in on the victorious sprinter, I expected her to flash that characteristic huge smile of hers. To my surprise, a look almost like sadness swept over her face. She brushed back the hood of her racing suit, sat down on the track just across the finish line, and cried. It didn't seem to be entirely a cry of joy. It seemed a cry of exhaustion and relief.

Sometimes that happens just after a great battle has been won. You're spent, exhausted. You just want to sit down and cry. Sometimes you even want to quit.

One of the amazing Bible stories to me has to do with how quickly Elijah's victory on Mt. Carmel turns to depression. As victory moments go, you don't get much better than this. It was a huge victory, but now Jezebel is after him. Elijah fears for his life and runs. He crawls under the shade of a broom tree and says to God, "I have had enough. Just take my life."[10]

How could he go from boldness to despair in such a short time? I think James gives us the answer. He says of Elijah: "He was a man just like us" (James 5:17). Just like us. Have you ever been in a place like that? Ever "had it" with life? Ever felt depressed even after a great spiritual victory?

There is a high cost to obedience, you know. The kind of stuff Jesus is asking us to be involved in is high cost. It can take everything from us. And that's where we find Elijah. From *hero* to *basket case* in a day.

There are at least two lessons to take from this narrative. One is how God met Elijah in his exhaustion. God refuses to accept Elijah's resignation. In fact, he gets Elijah back to work by giving him more to do. God's therapy for burnout is not only a retreat in the mountains. It also includes the assignment of a new task and the promise of a future. I learned this from Gene Getz's book, *Elijah: Remaining Steadfast Through Uncertainty.*

But God doesn't start there. First he meets this worn-out prophet right where he is. Isn't that good news? Sleep, nourishing food, fresh water to drink. Breathe out. Renew. Sabbath. You've got to have it. And in this place of rest, the Lord broadened Elijah's perspective by telling him that he never expected him to bear Israel's problems all by himself. He's going to have help, but God won't let him resign. Rest? *Yes.* Resignation? *No.*

There seems to be a belief these days that God would never really expect us to pour out all of our life's energy on ministry. We used to sing a song years ago "Let me burn out for Thee, O Lord." Now we are kind of embarrassed by that idea.

Truth is, the cost of obedience is tremendous. So it's not unusual to come to a place like Elijah did. And in those moments we need renewal to be sure. But that's not the end of the story, and it's not the point of the story. Sooner or later, God says, "All right—get up now. It's time to get on with it."

Sometimes people who love me scold me about having so many responsibilities. I appreciate that. I really do. And I want to have a balanced and healthy life. I don't think for a moment that the salvation of the world depends on me.

But at the same time, I don't want to come face-to-face with the Lord on the final day knowing that I've held back. The cost of total obedience is high. It'll take your life. I've decided that by God's grace it's a price I'm willing to pay. How about you?

WHEN YOU FEEL
OVERWHELMED

So how often do you feel totally overwhelmed with the realities of being a pastor? That often, huh? Me too. There's just no way around it—this is a big job that God has asked us to do. The life of a pastor is full of tasks and responsibilities that stretch the limits of our ability.

Do you think it's a spiritual principle that God delights in calling us to tasks that are too big for us? One of the "icons" on my office wall regularly reminds me of this truth. It says, "Nothing is more pathetic than having a big assignment and a small character."

Whenever I think about this, I take some comfort from remembering the life of Moses. You know all about the amazing plan that God developed for freeing His people from Egypt. Moses thought it was a great plan too—until the other shoe dropped. God delineates his great plan and then says to Moses, "So now, go. I am sending *you* to do this." Suddenly Moses isn't quite so impressed with the plan. He raises five objections to the Lord. I wonder if they sound at all familiar to you?

First, Moses says, "Who am I?" He protests God's plan because he has no authority, no position of power from which to exert the influence needed to pull this thing off.

Basically God's answer to that objection is "You don't have to be anybody important or powerful, because I will be with you."

So Moses raises his second objection: "Who are you?" How's that for foolish courage? Moses is really saying here, "God, I don't know you well enough to speak for you." God's answer back is simple: "When you go, just tell them that you come in the name of 'I AM'—that's all you need."

Third objection. Moses says, "Well that's good, but just in case they still don't believe me, what then?" So God gives Moses some amazing signs and wonders to perform as proof that he comes in the name of the Lord.

Fourth objection. "God, I don't talk so well." Now that one

amazes me. He protests that he can't go and be God's mouthpiece before Pharaoh because he is slow of speech. But for the past 20 verses he sure has been mouthing off to God! So the Lord says, "Listen, don't you worry about your speaking ability. I made your mouth—I can make it work right."

Fifth objection. Now we get to the real stuff. "Lord, isn't there someone else who can do it?" That is the bottom line. He sees the risk, and he wants out. Just as soon as Moses gets out that fifth objection, we hear the scariest word of this whole passage: "Then the LORD's anger burned against Moses" (Exodus 4:14). That can't be good. But God in his graciousness says to Moses, "All right. Listen, if you are afraid of this big assignment I'll send your brother to help you."

I think Moses learned a critical lesson that day. The bush should have been the first clue. The fire was to get Moses' attention—a visible sign of God's presence. It didn't need the bush to burn, but God chose to use a bush in order to get Moses' attention. I think it was Dennis Kinlaw I heard say once, "God needs a bush, and any old bush will do." Because the power is not in the bush—it's in the presence of the Lord.

God has a bigger-than-life assignment for every one of us. The good news is that when God chooses you, it's never about being capable for the task. It's always about being available. Ask yourself if you are at a place in your spiritual life where you are willing to say to the Lord, whenever he calls and whatever the assignment, "Here I am, Lord. I am totally available to you." Maybe "overwhelmed" isn't such a bad state for a pastor. It may help us remember to rely on the power of the Sender.

ANGER IN THE PASTOR'S STUDY

It has become so commonplace that it hardly shocks us anymore. Our news is filled with it every day. The unexpected, unforeseen explosion of an angry person often leaves some dead, others grieving, many hurt, and all of us bewildered. This is an age of rage.

We who are on the front lines of serving people know the destruction that comes to individuals and families because of unbridled anger. Yet how often do we deal with intense feelings of anger that are directly linked to our profession? Let me explain.

Have you ever had someone tell you he or she was leaving the church because he or she wasn't being fed adequately? Have you ever uncovered gossip about you or someone in your family? Have you ever stepped off the platform after a wonderful service of worship when the presence of the Lord was so near, only to have someone come up and in about three seconds suck all the joy right out of you?

In the work that you and I do, we have ample opportunity to follow the advice of James: "Be quick to listen, slow to speak, and slow to become angry" (James 1:19). We know anger is not good for us, but we sometimes seem nearly powerless to stop it. We sense the wisdom of James' words, but how regularly do we actually live them out?

It helps me to broaden my perspective beyond particular relationships and remember the kind of culture in which I am living and working. Speaking broadly, "nothing is clear anymore. Not job security, nor the point of our ambitions, nor marital permanence, nor sex roles, parenting styles, social etiquette, medical advice, not even basic news which comes at us from so many sources that it contradicts and overwhelms us."[11]

We are on edge. We are anxious. And that converts to anger. Why? Because anger is a more tolerable human emotion than fear is. And fear is the real culprit. We are dealing with people who are fearful, and we as pastors even deal with it. Many of us are afraid that if we don't do well in our calling we will have no value as persons. Far too often we equate positive feedback with personal competency. Perhaps our fears are based in job security or even in a need to be "right."

What's the answer? I hope this doesn't come across as a simplistic answer, but I do believe that our theology gives us an answer as expressed in 1 John 4. "Perfect love drives out fear." Perfect love is not our doing. It's God's. And it comes out of a life of total surrender.

The only way that I have discovered to help me deal with the things that lead to anger is to live daily in full surrender to the lordship of Jesus Christ. When I do, then when I hear criticism, my response is not self-justification but the realization that often a critical spirit comes from that person's pain and has nothing to do with me. When I live in surrender to Christ, I can release my need to be right, trusting God, who knows my heart, to validate my ministry. When I am fully surrendered to Christ, my value and esteem are found in Him and not in whether my board thinks I am doing a good job.

So the next time you deal with what H. B. London calls a "joy-sucker," maybe your focus should not be on why you are angry but rather why you are fearful. What fear is standing in the way of loving those who hurt and frustrate us with God's perfect love?

FAITHFUL DOUBTERS

How much faith is enough faith for Jesus to change your life?

One man simply cried out in desperate fear, "Jesus, son of David, have mercy on me!" Jesus asked him what he wanted. He said, "I want to see again." That's it. No statement of faith in Jesus as the Christ, no confession of his belief. But that day he went from blindness to sight (Mark 10).

Another man said, "I can't get into the healing pool when the waters are stirred. Someone else always beats me to it. They get the miracle and I remain lame. Thirty-eight years!" That's all he said to Jesus. Didn't ask to be healed. Never said, "Jesus, I believe that you can heal me. I have faith in you." He just said, "My life is broken." And Jesus healed him and sent him on his way a changed man (John 5).

How much faith is enough faith for Jesus to change your life?

Over and over again in the Gospels this kind of story is told. The lives of people are changed when it seems that they have little faith. One of my favorite stories is the one about the father in Mark 9. His servant was dying, and he asked Jesus to heal him. He said to Jesus, "If . . . if you can do anything."

Jesus said to this father, "Everything is possible for him who believes." Doesn't that make it sound like God's intervention in your life is dependent on your faith? If I really believe, good things happen. If I don't truly believe—forget it!

"I do believe," he said. "Help me overcome my unbelief!" Apparently just that much faith is enough. Do you ever struggle with doubts in your Christian walk? Do you ever worry that your faith is weak and wanting? I know that I'm talking to pastors and leaders of the Church, but some of the greatest leaders in our own tradition have struggled with doubts. John Wesley struggled for a long time, being convinced of his unbelief. Phineas Bresee's main spiritual struggle was with doubt. This is not about an unbelief that rejects the authority of Jesus. This is about the honest struggles that come with trying to connect what is with what the gospel promises.

There is nothing wrong with faithful doubt and honest struggle.

It is possible to be a faithful doubter. I love the story that Annie Dillard tells about a little church that she sometimes attends. One Sunday the pastor was leading the congregation in prayers of intercession, pretty much the same list as usual. Suddenly, in the midst of the rather routine prayer, the pastor burst out in an agitated voice, "Lord, we bring these same petitions every week!" Annie Dillard writes, "Because of this, I like him very much."[12]

Faith is not a feeling or the absence of doubt. Faith is a matter of divine grace. Faith is surrender to the authority of Jesus. Pastor, do you ever struggle with faith? I know it would be hard for you to admit that to anyone. However, I invite you to bring the struggle to Jesus with the faithful cry of the father in Mark 9, Lord, "I do believe; help me to overcome my unbelief!"

CAN A PASTOR
KEEP THE SABBATH?

My daughter's fifth-grade Sunday School class was studying the Ten Commandments. One Sunday afternoon at the dinner table I asked her what she was learning. She very proudly reported that they had studied the fourth commandment that day: "Remember the Sabbath day, by keeping it holy." Like any good parent, I asked, "Do you know what that means?" She replied confidently, "Yep, it means you don't work on Sunday but rest, because on the seventh day God rested." I applauded her comprehension. But then she asked me, "So, Dad, why don't *you* keep the Sabbath?" Ouch!

Her question was quite well founded. Already, for the first 11 years of her life, she had observed me Sunday after Sunday pour out everything I had until I crashed in a lifeless heap on the family room couch late Sunday night.

The realities of pastoral life make Sabbath-keeping a real challenge, but keep it we must! If we are to avoid the much-dreaded "pastoral burnout syndrome," we had better pay close attention to the biblical pattern of work and rest. I've always affirmed this truth yet too often found myself chief among Sabbath violators.

Pastors are notorious for talking about how busy they are. I've had colleagues tell me that they hadn't taken a day off in weeks and hadn't really taken a vacation in years. I think they wanted me to be impressed with their commitment. I was saddened instead.

Henri Nouwen writes that we seem to take "being busy and being important . . . to mean the same thing."[13] We rush about trying to prove our worth through our frenetic activity. Truth is, many of our people have no idea what we really do with our time. They have no comprehension of why we often put in 70- and 80-hour weeks trying to balance it all. But that's no excuse for trying to prove our competency to them by working so hard that it leaves us exhausted.

In his wonderful book *The Contemplative Pastor*, Eugene H. Peterson writes, "The adjective *busy* set as a modifier to *pastor* should sound to our ears like *adulterous* to characterize a wife or *embezzling* to describe a banker. It is an outrageous scandal, a blasphemous affront."[14]

God built the rhythms of work and rest into our very beings and into the natural world. We ignore these rhythms to our physical, emotional, and spiritual detriment. I assume that God was quite serious when he commanded his people to rest one day out of the week. Who am I to think I can ignore this basic command and still provide adequate spiritual leadership to my family as well as to my congregation?

Peterson goes on to suggest some practical steps for making Sabbath spaces in our lives. "The trick . . . is to get to the calendar before anyone else does. I mark out the times for prayer, for reading, for leisure, for the silence and solitude out of which creative work . . . can issue. I find that when these central needs are met, there is plenty of time for everything else."[15]

So how are you doing at keeping the Sabbath? What steps do you need to take in order to establish true Sabbath rest in your weekly schedule? Take one step this week. You need the rest.

THE PASTOR'S PRIVATE LIFE

Our families see it best of all. The sudden snap out of a bad mood when a church member calls on the telephone. The teacher of spiritual disciplines being too tired to pray. The patient counselor lashing out at a disobedient son or daughter.

Granted, a degree of this disparity in our public and private lives is normal. After all, every person tends to "let down" at home a bit differently than he or she does in public. The problem comes when we allow a chasm to develop between what our people see and believe about our spiritual health and the truth about how healthy we indeed are.

Statistics and personal stories are bearing out that as pastors we deal with a load of spiritual disease that we tend to keep very private. The issues may range from anger to addictions, but too often we find a big difference between the person who stands in the pulpit on Sunday and the person we see in the mirror on Monday morning.

What does it take to live as people of truth and integrity? Our public life calls us to have it all together, yet we are real, growing, sometimes struggling followers of Jesus. At times we are last to admit the incongruity. Author Fred Smith, in his article "Conducting a Spiritual Audit" that appeared in *Leadership Journal* in Winter 1998, offers some good questions we can ask ourselves that will help us evaluate our spiritual health. Here are a few of the questions he suggests that can help us conduct a personal spiritual audit:

First, am I content with who I am becoming? Each day I move one step closer to the person I will ultimately become. Am I satisfied with the direction things are moving in my private life?

Am I becoming less religious and more spiritual? Does my spirituality revolve around the public acts of preaching, teaching, and leading in worship, or do those priestly acts flow out of a genuine spirituality that is being nurtured in the private places of my life?

Does my family recognize the authenticity of my spirituality? One well-known pastor said it this way: "I am weary of celebrity religion. I have had my share of honors, but when I die, unless my family can say, 'There is something of God in the man,' then I will have failed." If you really want to know the degree of integrity between your private and public life, just ask your spouse or your children.

Do I have a quiet center to my life? We are called on to do so many things and to be involved in so many people's lives that we leave no space for solitude. Busyness has become a debilitating disease for contemporary Christians, and often pastors are sickest of all. If there is no obvious place in my weekly schedule for retreat, recreation, and reflection, then I am probably not moving in a healthy spiritual direction.

The critical question is, *Am I honestly evaluating the congruity between who I know I am and who I seem to be in the eyes of others?* One of the most dangerous temptations for pastors is to allow a bifurcation to continue between our public and private lives. Don't let it happen. If it is happening, find someone to whom you can tell the truth about yourself and who can give you wise counsel on how to become a person of spiritual integrity.

WHEN SOMEONE THROWS DIRT ON YOUR HEAD

Of all the wonderful stories that come to us in the Bible surrounding the life of David, one of my favorites is in chapter 16 of 2 Samuel. The picture there is comical, but the lesson is grave.

When David finally comes to power and Saul is gone, things go very well for David's reign. However, there comes a point that he apparently forgets what he has learned about the dangers of abusing power. In fact, the problem of abusing power comes very close to home. In the sordid episode between Amnon, Tamar, and Absalom, David's reign begins to unravel until ultimately he loses the throne and flees Jerusalem in disgrace. That's when we are introduced to one, Shimei, who runs along the road with the deposed king and his entourage, shouting curses at David, pelting him with stones, and showering him with dirt (2 Samuel 16:5-13).

That's dangerous activity. You don't throw dirt on the king and get away with it. The secret service wanted to cut Shimei's head off, and David could have easily ordered it or at least allowed it. Instead, something happens that is rather remarkable to me. David receives these curses from Shimei as a word from the Lord. He said, "Leave him alone; let him curse, for the Lord has told him to do so" (2 Samuel 16:11).

Across more than 20 years now of pastoral ministry I have found myself sneaking back to this text now and again in the privacy of my study. It raises a contemporary and compelling question for me: "What is my reaction when a word of correction comes?" I do believe that the Lord sometimes uses people to speak correction into my life. And sometimes it feels rather like getting dirt thrown on my head. How do I react when the Lord's correction comes through a sod-throwing nut? Is there enough spiritual maturity in me that I can receive the corrective, harsh, even judgmental words of another as a possible word from the Lord?

I'll tell you what I'm tempted to do when harsh words come to me: I am tempted to dismiss the messenger. *Well that's just so and so—he's just a cranky person. He wouldn't be happy if Jesus was his pas-*

tor! I am tempted to look for a counter-charge: *How dare they say that about me when I know that they . . .* I am tempted to retreat and deny. I am tempted to harbor anger.

Granted, there are times when people confront and accuse us and the problem really is theirs, not ours. But we'd better be careful, because sometimes the Lord just might want to speak to us through some nut throwing dirt on our heads. David understood this. I believe it is part of what made him a great man in spite of his frail humanity. It's part of why in spite of his sin, he can be described as a man after God's own heart. He wasn't so hardened that he was unwilling to be challenged and to learn. And he learned enough to know that sometimes God may even use an angry, dirt–throwing pest to speak to us.

So the next time someone throws dirt on your head, "Be quick to listen, slow to speak and slow to become angry" (James 1:19). Allow the Lord to speak to you even through those who throw dirt.

WHEN CONGREGATIONS ABUSE PASTORS

Author David Hansen suggests that there are some churches that simply don't deserve a pastor. He describes what far too many pastors have experienced:

> Churches such as these disembowel pastors. With words as sharp as knives, they slice open a pastor's soul until the *splaxna* gushes out. They rip open the pastor's *racham*. They take *philos* but they cannot return it. They only know how to take. They are buckets without bottoms. No matter how much *hesed* you pour into them, it never hits bottom. They never fill up. They never overflow with love, mission, worship, or joy. They hate God's anointed. They despise the lordship of Christ, and they despise his ambassadors. They are spiritual anarchists.[16]

Wow! Tough words. Are they true? Are there some congregations that have so adulterated what it means to be "church" that they have fallen into a pattern of pastor abuse? Anecdotal evidence would confirm that this exists. Sad stories abound of pastors having been chewed up and spit out by ruthless people who have so taken control of some congregations that their anti-Christ attitude and behavior is allowed to rule. Some churches have even earned a reputation of being "pastor killers." What are the marks of such a group? I would define four based on David Hansen's observations of this phenomenon:

The first is a failure to submit to authority. The people in our churches today have been well schooled in resisting authority. The individual reigns in our culture. The problem is that, although people long for genuine community, there is no community without healthy authority.

The second is the habit of careless words. Ephesians 4 is quite clear that a congregation's failure to discipline its speech is deadly (Ephesians 4:29-32). Sins of the tongue will be evident in any group of people, even in Christian groups. However, when gossip and its family becomes rampant, the church is in serious trouble.

The third is a condition of prayerlessness. Each of us knows that when prayer fades from our personal discipline, our spiritual health also fades. If you want to know something about the health of a congregation, find out about its habits of prayer.

The fourth is a history of raising its hand against God's anointed. This history should not be ignored. When churches have a decades-long pattern of running off pastors, something must be done to bring that congregation to accountability. Denominational leaders have a major responsibility in this.

So what should you do when you discover that you are attempting to shepherd an abusive congregation? It is true that some churches don't deserve the love of a pastor, but that does not translate to a one-way ticket out of town for you. It may be that your work in that place is to break a pattern of abuse, to name the sinful behavior, and to faithfully preach and teach the biblical vision of community. There is no doubt that the price for such a ministry is high.

There are times when you will have to follow Jesus' advice to "shake the dust off your feet when you leave" (Mark 6:11). But you did not choose this vocation so that your life could be full of affirmation and comfort. You were chosen to be a sign of Christ's presence in the midst of a rebellious people. Remember the Lord's instruction to Ezekiel: "Whether they listen or fail to listen . . . they will know that a prophet has been among them" (Ezekiel 2:5). May the Lord give you grace to be a pastor, even when it means that you must bear "the marks of Jesus" (Galatians 6:17). The peace of Christ be with you.

FAILURE

Things that go together: Peanut butter and jelly, springtime and rain, Abbott and Costello, the Cubs and . . . well, you get the idea. How about failure and success?

Michael Jordan is recognized as one of the greatest athletes of all time. Listen to what he said, however, about his success: "I have missed more than 9,000 shots in my career. I have lost almost 300 games. On 26 occasions I have been entrusted to take the game winning shot, and I missed. I have failed over and over and over again in my life. And that's precisely why I succeed."[17]

The way we respond to failure says a lot about us. Some people have the ability to use failure as a catalyst, while others are crushed by it. Psychologist Perry Buffington writes about something called the "Zeigarnik effect." It's when our failures begin to take on a life of their own, because the brain remembers incomplete tasks longer than a completed activity. "Failures have no closure. The brain continues to spin the memory, trying to come up with ways to fix the mess and move it from active to inactive status."

If you have ever lain awake at night running a misstep through your mind over and over again, then you understand the effect. There is an important question to face at this point: Will I live in fear of failing again and become paralyzed, or will I allow this failure to become a tool in God's hand to shape my life?

It seems to me that this is a decision we pastors are compelled to make multiple times in our vocational life. The work of pastor is risky business and fraught with opportunity for failure. But who decides what constitutes failure? Does society judge my work as failure or success? Does the congregation decide? My family? Is it up to me to decide? Maybe the more important question, no matter how well or how poorly I think things are going, is this: How is God in this moment shaping my character in the image of Christ Jesus?

Brennan Manning in his wonderful book *The Wisdom of Tenderness* puts it like this: "It's more important to be a mature Christian than to be a great butcher or baker or candlestick-maker; and if the only chance to achieve the first is to fail at the second, the failure will have proved worthwhile."[18]

I wonder if this is what the writer of Hebrews had in mind while penning the words "No discipline seems pleasant at the time, but painful. Later on, however, it produces a harvest of righteousness and peace for those who have been trained by it. Therefore, strengthen your feeble arms and weak knees. Make level paths for your feet, so that the lame may not be disabled, but rather healed" (Hebrews 12:11-13).

My friend, if you are struggling with a sense of failure just now, if you are feeling beaten down and defeated by circumstances that have turned out badly, please remember that God is working toward the good. Maybe an important part of the process is a decision that you can make. Will you respond to this failure only as a defeat and embarrassment? Or will you allow God to redeem the failure into the most lasting kind of success?

WHEN IT'S TIME TO LEAVE

His question took me back. I was getting ready to spend several weeks studying how pastors can lengthen their local tenure. I had interviews lined up and questionnaires prepared. And then he hit me with his question. "So what about when it's time to leave? How does a pastor know that? Sometimes pastors stay too long, you know. It can really damage a church."

It made me think. As I spent the next several weeks trying to learn how to stay, his question was never far behind. Beyond being forced out by a dysfunctional congregation, how *does* a pastor know when it's time to move on?

I reflected on and prayed over that question, and several things came to mind. I remembered that on a number of occasions in the Bible God chose different leaders for different times. Clearly communities of faith have "seasons" in their corporate lives. Maybe God intends there to be different leaders in the various seasons. Also, if I truly believe that I am called by God, is it too naive to think that he will give me clear direction when it's time to go? If so, how does he make that direction known to me? I identified four strategies that I want to employ when making this critical decision.

1. If it's time to move on, there is probably another opportunity for service awaiting me. If I really believe that God is guiding this process, then am I willing to take a lack of offers as a sign to stay put? We need to be exceedingly cautious about putting resumes out in order to engineer a move.

2. The potential move needs to seem "good to the Holy Spirit and to us" (Acts 15:28). Of course, the context of this statement was the community of faith. Somehow God's will was made known to them as they processed the questions *together*. Could it be that we pastors need to be courageous enough to invite one or two trusted laypersons into this process early on?

3. There needs to be time and dialogue between pastor and people before a change like this takes place. I realize I'm going out on a limb here, because this is a different paradigm than what we are used to. Usually pastors take great pains to go through this process in secret. But if we really believe what we say we believe about being family with our congregations, then why wouldn't we allow this to be a family discussion? Pastors often talk of being released from an assignment when the people certainly don't feel released. Maybe this kind of dialogue could prevent some of the moves that we later regret.

4. **I concluded that my default answer to congregations that try to call me to another assignment needs to be "No, thank you. I already have an assignment."**

I guess the bottom line is that if I am part of a congregation that is seeking to be an authentic expression of the kingdom of God, I should trust them to help me answer this question. Our answer might be "Yes, it's time for a change." Or it could be "No, let's keep growing together." Either way, wouldn't it be healthier for everyone?

The Pastor as Prophet

ARE YOU A PESKY PROPHET?

Micaiah couldn't catch a break. He lived in service to a king that he could not please, no matter what he did. Micaiah could have made things easier on himself save for one truth: He knew that ultimately he lived in service to One much greater than Israel's king.

The story is told in 1 Kings 22. Aram and Israel were living in a three-year period of peace. King Ahab of Israel knew that peace is a highly overrated political asset, so during a visit with Jehoshaphat of Judah, he suggested some potential work for the military. It seems the Arameans were occupying a city that Israel claimed, and Ahab wanted to know if Jehoshaphat would join him to win back the real estate.

Jehoshaphat thought it sounded like a pretty good idea but wanted first to "find out what the Lord says" (v. 5, NLT). Good move. So Ahab called his prophets and asked whether or not they should go to war. You can see them falling all over themselves to tell the king what he wants to hear: "Go right ahead! The Lord will give you a glorious victory!" (v. 6). Jehoshaphat knew theirs was not an authoritative word. So he asked, "Isn't there a prophet of the Lord around, too? I would like to ask him the same question" (v. 7). Here is where the vocational integrity of Micaiah was revealed. Ahab said, "There is still one prophet of the Lord, but I hate him. He never prophesies anything but bad news for me! (v. 8).

Sometimes when people don't like our preaching it's because we're not doing a very good job of it. There are other times, however, when people don't like our preaching because the truth of God's word cuts across their compromised lives.

The kings called Micaiah on the carpet. They were decked out in their official garb, and the prophets of Ahab were there with the prophetic smoke and mirrors that impresses kings. The messenger who went to get Micaiah told him on the way to the court, "Look, all the prophets are promising victory for the king. Be sure that you agree with them and promise success" (v. 13). Micaiah came before Ahab, and the king asked the question, "Should we go to war against Ramoth-gilead or not?" Micaiah said, "Go right ahead! The Lord will give the king a glorious victory!" (v. 15). Did the prophet sell out? Well, King Ahab saw right through the sarcastic agreement of Micaiah. He barked impatiently at Micaiah, "How many times must I demand that you speak only the truth when you speak for the Lord?" (v. 16). So Micaiah got serious. He painted a grim picture for the king of what would happen if he pursued this course of action. It was not good news. It seems that Ahab already knew deep inside that it would not be good news, for he knew he was living in disobedience to the Lord. So he lashed out, "Didn't I tell you? He does it every time. He never prophesies anything but bad news for me" (v. 18). And he had Micaiah thrown into prison with nothing but bread and water to sustain him. Actually, Micaiah had a sustenance that Ahab could not understand. He revealed his true heart to the messenger when he said, "As surely as the Lord lives, I will say only what the Lord tells me to say" (v. 14).

Pastor, what will you say to your people this Sunday? Will you be able to resist the frightening description of 2 Timothy 4:3? It says, "For a time is coming when people will no longer listen to right teaching. They will follow their own desires and will look for teachers who will tell them whatever they want to hear." Or will you have the courage to fulfill your calling and proclaim the truth of God? Are you willing, if the Lord leads, to become a pesky prophet to a complacent and compromised people? May the Lord bless and strengthen you, Pastor, as you stand in the pulpit to tell the truth.

how does one preach truth faithfully?

WE ARE CHRISTIAN

I am grateful that when our Board of General Superintendents gave expression to our core values, they started with the simple statement "We are a Christian People." This may seem painfully obvious, but in the life of our local congregations it often is not obvious. There is a tendency in local Nazarene congregations to define church life by a much shallower story than the historic Christian faith.

We have a deep and rich heritage that gives shape to our life and ministry today. Our immediate heritage is the Holiness revival that swept North America in the latter part of the 19th century. Much of who we are and how we "do church" certainly comes out of this modern movement. The vitality of our worship, the presence of the "mourner's bench" (altar), the common "invitation" to pray the sinner's prayer, and many other Nazarene features are gifts to us from our Holiness revival heritage. But our story is much deeper than that. Our faith and practice have roots that go all through the story of God's people called the Church.

We confess that we are part of the "one, holy, universal, and apostolic" Church. We identify with the story of God's people throughout 20 centuries of Christian history. We see our roots even in the Old Testament story of God working to redeem his chosen people. We understand that our theology has been shaped by the doctrinal expressions of the Early Church as they sought to articulate their faith. We are deeply marked by the Protestant Reformation and by the Wesleyan revival of the 18th century. Our story is long and deep and significant.

So what difference does all this make now? Let me suggest just a few ways that I believe it makes a difference in my pastoral work.

Remembering our deep roots helps me to guide my people when they are tempted to define the kingdom of God by a nationalistic vision of a Christian America. The voices of the saints through the ages teach me that salvation does not come through a government that gives freedom to the Church. The only hope of salvation is through a Redeemer who works through his Body to reconcile the world to himself. Consequently, our primary energy is not given to making the systems of government, education, and business work right. Our primary work is to announce to people the good news of how Jesus can make them right, which will in turn impact the world.

When I try to teach my people to understand the significance of baptism, I know that I am helping them connect to Christians through the ages. These forbearers understood the sacrament as more than a personal testimony—as a vital means of God's grace.

When I guide my congregation in marking time by the Christian year instead of by the civil calendar, we are all reminded that the story of God's work in Christ is not something we just lately figured out how to preach. Indeed, the historic Christian faith gives us the language of faith as we rehearse the Christ-story through Advent, Christmas, Epiphany, Lent, Easter, and Pentecost.

These are just three simple examples of how important it is to me that we identify ourselves not only by 100 years of denominational history but also by 2,000 years of Christian history. Though we Nazarenes understand our distinct mission in the world with regard to the Holiness message, we are first of all Christian. And a major part of our pastoral task is to teach our people that truth.

DOES ANYBODY REALLY KNOW WHAT TIME IT IS?

Horace Whittel, a dockworker in Gillingham, England, hated his alarm clock. Every working day for 47 years, its bell had jarred Horace awake. Every day, he wished he could ignore it. Finally Whittel got his revenge. On the day he retired, his alarm clock jolted him awake as usual, but this time he took the clock with him to the dockyards where he worked. With a mischievous grin on his face, he placed his alarm under an 80-ton hydraulic press and pushed the button. Horace laughed with delight at seeing his old enemy flattened.

Wouldn't you love to do that tomorrow morning? Our world pushes us to fill every available space of life. I am constantly amazed at how many different activities my teenagers can cram into one evening. The clear call of our world is to do more, be more, experience more, give more, go more, buy more, love more—more, more, more!

In Matthew 16 Jesus speaks to some folks very much like us about the issue of time. He says, "You know how to predict and interpret a lot of natural things, but you don't have a clue about how to discern the signs of the times."

In Jesus' language there were a few different words for time. One of them was *chronos,* which is the kind of time we are most aware of. *Chronos* time is linear. It's the duration of temporal time, or the passing of hours, days, and weeks. It's what our alarm clocks and calendars keep track of. However, the word Jesus uses for time in this passage is a different word: *kairos. Kairos* time means a significant event in a moment of time.

What Jesus was saying to his audience is that they could see *chronos* time very well, but they were blind to *kairos* time. In other words, their lives were being defined by their own temporal, short-sighted way of looking at things. So much so that they could not even see what God was doing right in front of their faces.

We can become so consumed with *chronos* time that we totally miss the *kairos* of what God would like to do for us. I think what

Jesus would say to us is, "Don't become so consumed by the *chronos* that you miss the *kairos.*

Don't become so expert at fulfilling all the obligations and expectations that you miss the new and simple ways that God would like to show himself to you."

What ways is he talking about? It has been my experience that it comes in the simple, not in the spectacular. It might be in a moment of quiet. It might be in a moment of corporate worship. It might be in the face of a child. It might be in a simple pastoral conversation with someone who is hurting.

Pastor-friend, there is a way to live without being choked to death by time, by alarm clocks, by schedules, by pressures. Oh, we will always deal with those things, but they truly do not have to define our lives. The good news is that we can allow Jesus to re-tune our hearts and minds to the *kairos* of our lives. We can be attentive to activities of the Spirit, so that the activities of the world don't choke the life out of us.

Which time are you paying attention to? Is your life so consumed by *chronos* that you can't see the *kairos*? May the Spirit of Christ capture your heart and help you to see what time it really is.

WHAT TO DO
ABOUT ORNERY PEOPLE

It's getting to where I open my E-mail with one eye peeking through my fingers, afraid to see what the electronic dumping ground may bring today. It's an occupational hazard, I guess. When you open your mouth to talk for more than five minutes at a time, sooner or later someone is going to get offended.

Two episodes come to mind. Several years ago I was leading our congregation in the reciting of the Apostles' Creed. We spoke in unison, "I believe in . . . the holy catholic Church . . ." First thing Monday morning I had a call from a man that was new to our congregation. For ten minutes He unleashed on me an angry tirade over the fact that we had identified ourselves as catholic. My explanations fell on deaf ears, and he finally slammed down the receiver in anger.

Episode number two. While preaching on God's power to heal, I made a statement that sounded like I was condemning all use of prescription drugs for mental health. The next day I received a strong but polite E-mail from a man in my congregation challenging my statement.

My feelings in both of those situations were similar, even though the approach was different. In the first, the individual's criticism was based on false understanding. More than that, he was unwilling to hear my explanation. You can't reason with irrational people.

In the second situation, the man who challenged my statement was absolutely correct to do so. I learned some important lessons about how careful I need to be with generalizations. I realized that, even though I intended no harm, harm was done, and I had to take responsibility for it. Many of the feelings were the same. At first I felt defensive and embarrassed. I wanted to shoot back, "That's not what I meant!" Instead, I asked forgiveness for my carelessness and chalked up a crucial lesson.

My point is that when we are criticized, it is vital that we take time to understand what is really behind that criticism. Our feelings are often the same regardless of the motives of the criticizer. It takes a little time to sort through the feelings so that we can get to the truth or error of the person's critique.

I have learned a couple of things that help me with this process. First I ask myself, "Who is this criticizer?" Is this a person who habitually finds something to complain about? Or is this a person who speaks criticism judiciously? That doesn't mean I can always dismiss the words of the habitual criticizer, but it does begin to help me hear the criticism more objectively.

Second, I ask myself, "What about this criticism is true?" Even in the most outrageous of allegations there can be an element of truth that I need to hear.

Third, I often ask someone else for his or her opinion. Obviously the issue of confidentiality needs consideration, but I generally run the criticism by my spouse, a staff member, a pastor-friend, or even a trusted layperson. Very often just repeating it aloud brings the resolution of my feelings and a new perspective on the issue.

Sometimes criticism comes from ornery people. Sometimes it comes from people who love us and want the best for us. What we do not have in pastoral ministry is the luxury of dismissing the ranting of ornery people. God uses ornery people to get my attention. He uses their criticism to remind me that I must do this job with humility and with absolute dependence on Him. He also reminds me that I do not have an option when it comes to loving those who are hard to love. And nothing teaches love faster than the challenge of loving a cantankerous saint.

THE INFORMATION/ACTION RATIO

The principal of our local middle school is on to something. In addition to the core curriculum, he arranges for his students to leave the school grounds during the day and spend time with local senior adults. They do practical things like baking cookies and planting gardens. The reason may be apparent, but I like how Mr. Neal expresses it.

"When we were kids we had lots of knowledge and a little information. Today's kids have more information than they know what to do with, but very little knowledge. Information is acquired through technology. Knowledge is acquired through relationships."

In this Internet age we are bombarded with more information that we can possibly process. Fifteen years ago I was incredulous at the notion that I could one day download the information of the world into my home or office. And yet here we are. Virtually any piece of information I want is available to me through my computer.

Having all this information at our disposal is in some ways a good thing. It also leads to a dangerous modern phenomenon. There is simply no way we can respond to all that we know, so in effect, we are being trained to do nothing about what we learn.

The main delivery mechanisms of this information, namely television and computers, further train us to passively receive loads of information without having to do much with it. It's mostly out of any relational context and rarely calls for any action from us. This produces in us a low information/action ratio. What we know is grossly out of proportion with what we *do* about what we know.

This idea was introduced to me by Marva Dawn in a retreat she and Eugene Peterson conducted for pastors. Marva outlines this problem in her wonderful book *Reaching Out Without Dumbing Down*. Here she notes the landmark work of Neil Postman and reflects on the implications of this malady for the church. She writes, "People are accustomed to 'learning' good ideas (even from sermons) and then doing nothing about them."[19]

Perhaps this gives us some insight as to why people don't seem to change much in response to God's truth. Our folks have been trained by culture not to feel too badly if they know a lot more than they live. That's why people can tell you with straight faces how wonderful the preaching is and how much they are learning, yet they don't ever seem to significantly incorporate the truth they are learning into their lives.

So what can be done about this? Let me suggest one simple pastoral strategy. We must be very specific with our people about the response the Bible is calling for. It's not enough to lay out a flawless explication of God's answer for the human dilemma without taking the next step and intentionally calling our people to some kind of specific response.

Sometimes the response is a prayer of repentance at the altar. Sometimes the response is receiving the sacrament of the Eucharist. At other times, we might call people to take a particular action during the next week like talking with an estranged relative or doing an act of kindness for a neighbor. Our people should leave every sermon with a clear understanding of how they could respond to the truth proclaimed. If we only preach the truth and do not find ways to hold our people accountable for response, we are doing less than our full pastoral work. Only the Holy Spirit can fully accomplish this task, but we are to be His instruments in helping our people to overcome their low information/action ratio.

Like our local middle school principal, teach the basics—but then help get your people out of the pew and into the world, putting into practice the high calling of life in the kingdom of God.

The Pastor as Priest

LET US WORSHIP GOD

One of my favorite visions of the Revelator is the scene in chapter four of worship around the throne of God. It makes me wonder about that day when all God's people are finally gathered around the throne of the Lamb.

Can you picture yourself there? I try to see it and hear it. As we are worshiping together, I can imagine that soon we hear the majestic strains of a great organ beginning to play, "All hail the power of Jesus' name." Suddenly a voice from the crowd shouts out, "Organ music! I hate organ music! It's old-fashioned and stale. Let's jazz this up a bit. Get the guitars and drums! Fire up the synthesizer!" So then we hear, in competition with the great organ, the lively sounds of a praise band. And suddenly other voices are raised, saying, "What is this sentimental drivel? This isn't real music." And the great throng before the throne divides between those who prefer traditional and those who prefer contemporary.

Then someone suggests, "Let's recite the 23rd Psalm together. And a chorus begins, "The Lord is my shepherd." But soon we hear another voice. "This is cold ritualism. Don't tell me what to say and when to say it. Let's be spontaneous in our worship." And the great throng divides again between those who prefer liturgy and those who prefer spontaneous praise.

Ridiculous picture, isn't it? How absurd to think that a great throng of worshipers who find themselves before the throne of Christ could ever become so self-focused. But wouldn't we have to admit that this is at least a somewhat accurate description of the Church today?

It's instructive to me that John doesn't spend one syllable describing the journey of those who worship and how they got there. It's all about the One who alone is worthy of worship.

The simple but important lesson we need to get about worship is that it is all about God and not about us. When my concern for a Sunday morning is whether or not I got something out of it, or "was fed," or enjoyed the service, I have missed the point. If my concern was whether or not I enjoyed the music, or the temperature was right, or the sound system worked—if those are the things that take my attention, I have not worshiped.

We must be diligent to keep the focus that in worship God is both the object and the subject.[20] We usually get one of those but not the other. I think we intuitively know that God is the object of worship, but it's amazing how often we make ourselves the subject. Just listen to how we sing and pray. Listen to how often our focus is on what we do, on what we bring, on what we need, on what we want from God.

Pastor, one of the most important things you can ever do in your congregation is to remind them week after week that worship is about God, not us. Say it, model it, plan the service to be faithful to it—this is all for God.

I had the privilege a few years back of visiting with Eugene Peterson about pastoral ministry. One of the things he said that day has locked in my memory: "If the only thing I ever did was stand before my people every week and say, 'Let us worship God,' I think I would have earned my salary."

I think he's right. Go earn your salary!

THIS IS THE
WORD OF THE LORD

Nazarenes have always had a high view of the Scriptures. Our worship centers on the reading of the Bible and the proclamation of its truth through preaching. We know that the Scriptures, faithfully proclaimed in the worshiping community, have a shaping influence on the life of that congregation. Lately I've been deeply concerned about reports that in an increasing number of Nazarene congregations, the Scriptures are not read, not even for the sermon. This practice does not accurately reflect who we are.

The selection of Scripture readings for the weekly worship of the church is a vital pastoral task. We don't want to select the scriptures to be read on the basis of personal taste or on the whim of the moment but on an intentional plan for helping our people to hear "the whole counsel of God."

One tool that is gaining wider acceptance in Nazarene circles is the lectionary. A lectionary is simply a collection of readings or selections from the Scriptures arranged and intended for proclamation during the worship of the church. Lectionaries have been around for a long time. Tables of readings were known and used in the fourth century, following the seasons and days of the Christian year from Advent to Pentecost. The lectionary provides a three-year plan or pattern for the Sunday readings. Each year is centered on one of the synoptic gospels. Year A is the year of Matthew, Year B is the year of Mark, and Year C is the year of Luke. John is read each year, especially in the times around Christmas, Lent, and Easter. Each week's selections generally include a lesson from the Old Testament, a selection from the Psalms, a Gospel reading, and an additional New Testament lesson. In the course of the three-year cycle the congregation will hear from a wide and balanced selection of Bible texts.

A few pastors use the lectionary to guide their preaching. Many others use the lectionary to choose readings for other parts of the worship service. It can also be used to develop Sunday School lessons, Bible studies, or even to guide the selection of music for the day. I have often used the lectionary to guide my devotional reading for the week.

The use of a lectionary doesn't need to be viewed as giving way to cold ritual or formalism. To the contrary, I have been amazed at how often the reading of a lection passage has precisely fit the need of the congregation on that particular day. There's nothing sacred about the lectionary. It's simply a tool that we can use to help guide our people to the Word of God in a way that will be intentional and comprehensive.

A number of different lectionaries are available. One that is widely used and has a very user-friendly format is *The Revised Common Lectionary* published by The Consultation on Common Texts.[21] There are also hundreds of Internet sites that include the lectionary readings for each Sunday.[22]

May I encourage you to check out a lectionary? You just might find it to be a useful tool in your careful pastoral work of facilitating the intersection of people's lives with the Word of God.

WORSHIP AT THE TABLE
With Thanks to William Willimon

One of my favorite Easter stories is about the two travelers of Emmaus Road as related in Luke 24. After the tragic events of Passover week, we find Cleopas and his friend dragging their weary bodies home, going over and over again the unbelievable events.

Suddenly another man joins them on that road. Luke tells us that it is the risen Christ, but for some reason the two disciples don't recognize him. So Jesus enters in to their dire conversation. The two spill their hearts to him about all that had just happened.

And then Jesus holds a Bible study right there on the Emmaus Road. He opens up the scriptures to them with his words and explains everything from Moses and the prophets that related to the coming Messiah. But still, they do not recognize him. Finally, they come to their exit and Jesus intends to move on down the road. The two travelers, however, convince him to come in and have supper with them.

It's at the table that things really change. For while he is at the table with them, he takes bread, gives thanks, breaks it, and passes it to them. Suddenly their eyes are opened, and they recognize that it is Jesus.

This whole story, it seems to me, is a picture of how our people come to worship. So often we find them coming on Sunday the way these two disciples were walking down that road—despondent, dejected, and defeated. The world is a tough place to live. So they come in with eyes closed, slow to see, slow to hear God's Word. But then, Christ calls us to his table. He takes the bread, blesses it, breaks it, gives it, and our eyes are opened!

Does this story challenge our common pattern for worship? We've always understood the Word as central to our worship. For us, the climactic point of the service is the proclamation of the gospel through preaching. The Word read, the Word preached, the Word studied and analyzed and listened to reigns supreme in our tradition. For many, communion has been seen as extra, even optional. Recent studies by Nazarene Research reveal that still nearly half of Nazarene congregations observe communion four or fewer times a year.[23] Obviously, we are less than convinced of the shaping significance of the Eucharist in our churches. But notice carefully what happens in the Gospel narrative. It was not in the proclamation of the Word, but in the sharing of the table that the eyes of these disciples were opened.

It's just like us. We come and we hear the ministry of the Word, we read our Bibles, we teach one another, but we do not always understand. We do not always see the presence of the Lord as a result of our hearing. And God, knowing that, invites us to move from word to deed. The word becomes act at the table. When we come in faith and see the breaking of the bread and share in the cup, somehow our eyes are opened, and we see the risen Christ in our midst.

Pastor-friend, we must understand how important the Lord's table is to what we are trying to accomplish. When we come together and partake, this sacramental moment loudly proclaims to us that all the promises and provisions of the Word are complete. They are *yes* and *amen* in Christ. Why would we offer that grace to our people only once a quarter? Why only once a month?

Some would say, "You have to be careful of having communion too much or it will become a dead ritual." Singing can become dead ritual, but we don't stop singing. Would communion become cold routine if we observed it more often? Five hundred years of Protestant church history would tell us otherwise. Overall, those churches with frequent communion tend to value it more than those whose coming to the table is sporadic.[24]

The act of coming to the Lord's Table is amazing grace. One of the most important pastoral acts we can offer to our people is to bring them to the table regularly. In the words of Charles Wesley, "Come, let us use the grace divine."

THE GIFT OF
PASTORAL BLESSING

One of my favorite moments in the worship service each Sunday morning is the benediction. I grew up pretty much thinking that *benediction* was simply a fancy word for "the last prayer before we get to go and eat." It's obviously much more. Benediction is a sacred opportunity that I have each week to lift my hands before the congregation and, as Christ's representative, offer a word of blessing to my people.

Often the words of the benediction come directly from Scripture as in the well-known priestly blessing of Numbers 6:25, "The Lord bless you and keep you; the Lord make his face shine upon you and be gracious to you; the Lord turn his face toward you and give you peace." Sometimes the blessing is from my own heart and related to the message of the day. This past Sunday, for example, I spoke these words after a message from Romans 12 on the nature of our relationship together as the Church: "May the Lord bless you with the ability to love one another. May God give you grace to live as reconcilers. And may we become a testimony to the world of the reconciling love of God in Christ."

Either way, I am convinced that this is far more than a "nice way to end the service." It is pastoral work. Somehow in the context of the worshiping congregation, those words are enabled by the Spirit to be life-giving for the people. Over time, the identity and health of a congregation can be shaped through the act of pastoral blessing.

Throughout the Bible, we see the power and importance of blessing. The covenant relationships that God shares with His people and that His people share with one another are relationships that are given shape and meaning through the act of blessing. One of the most poignant examples of the power of blessing is Esau crying to his father in desperation for a word of blessing in spite of his squandered inheritance (Genesis 27).

Our people live in a world that is filled with hurtful words. They receive messages every day of how inadequate they are. In a world based on competition and marked by violence, our people often come to worship with their Christian identity out of focus and their spiritual esteem damaged. As pastors, we have a great privilege and responsibility to remind them of who they really are in Christ. We can speak words to them that call them to reckon their lives according to the values of the kingdom of God rather than the kingdoms of this world.

Of course, benediction is not the only way to give pastoral blessing to people. We also do it in conversation with a person who is hurting. We do it when we kneel down to listen to the question of a child. It happens as we press the oil of anointing on the foreheads of those who have come for the prayer of healing. There are many ways to offer the blessing, but none is better than speaking words of grace and peace to our people who have gathered for worship. It may not seem on the surface like a very important act. I would suggest, however, that your people long for this kind of blessing from their pastor even if they wouldn't know how to name it.

May I encourage you to think intentionally about the ways you offer spiritual blessing to your people? Not only will they be blessed—so will *you!*

BEAR THE NAMES

I got bogged down in Exodus. One summer I was reading through the Exodus narrative during our family vacation. We were in the Desert Southwest of the United States, and as I sat outside reading and looking over the desert terrain, I could imagine the children of Israel wandering through Sinai.

However, I must confess that along about chapter 25 my eyes were reading the words, but my mind slipped off to the inviting waters of Lake Havasu. The details of the Tabernacle and its appointments got a bit repetitive and boring. But then, as so often happens, God jumped me in the midst of my dutiful reading.

In Exodus 28 the priestly garments for Aaron were being described in detail. They were beautiful and expensive. One of the details dictated to Moses had to do with two onyx stones on which he was to engrave the names of the sons of Israel. These stones were then to be placed in a gold setting and fastened to the shoulder pieces of the priest's ephod. Then the "breastpiece of decision" was described, also with twelve stones bearing the names of the sons of Israel. Why this detail? Here's the verse that pierced my heart: "Whenever Aaron enters the Holy Place, he will bear the names of the sons of Israel over his heart on the breastpiece of decision as a continuing memorial before the Lord" (Exodus 28:29).

Bear the names. Over his heart. Do I pray that way? Intercession for the people is a significant pastoral duty. I affirm that as do you, but this image of Aaron's priestly garment caused me to ask, "To what degree do I really bear the names of my people before the Lord?" When I pray for the congregation, do I pray in generic and collective ways? Do I pray for our outreach to the neighborhood? Do I pray for our programs? Do I pray that God will send revival to our Church? Those may all be good prayers, but how often do I bear the particular names of my people before the Lord?

This is good pastoral work. I might suggest some strategies for systematically engaging this work:

- Pray through the list of special needs. Each of our churches no doubt lists the particular requests and needs of people. This is an obvious place to begin.

- Pray through your appointment schedule. Pray with your calendar before you, and call the names of the people you've met with during the past week or that you anticipate meeting with in the coming week.
- Pray through the church directory. For some this may take a huge block of time and be possible only a few times a year. For others, you can do this weekly. I have noticed a real impact on my people when I report to them that I spent the better part of a particular day naming each of them in prayer.
- Pray for whomever the Spirit brings to mind. Sometimes I sit quietly before the Lord without a list in hand and just pray for the people who come to mind. It's amazing what I remember in these times about the needs of people that I did not have on my list.

Much of this is a mystery, but there is something powerful and good about a pastor naming his or her people before the Lord on a regular basis. And it's not only a task. God said about Aaron, "He will bear the names . . . over his heart." Pastor, whatever your strategy, "bear the names" from a heart of love for your people.

LET THE CHILDREN COME

All of us believe that children are a vital part of the Church. At least we say we believe that. We do seem to give great amounts of energy and resource to developing ministry and programs for children and their families. Many of our churches have hired children's ministry professionals to guide these vital efforts.

It's puzzling, then, that in far too many cases children continue to be marginalized in the life and worship of the Church. I wonder if some pastors and church leaders see children as a "ministry problem to be managed" rather than as an integral part of the community of faith. I actually heard about a pastor of a larger church who believes that children, by their very nature, are a distraction. I'm afraid this attitude is not uncommon. Let's see—what did Jesus say about that? I think he spoke to some folks (his disciples) who believed this also. I'm sure you remember the story from Mark 10, so I'll not go over it here. If memory serves me right, he said something about "do not hinder." I think the Gospel also says something on how Jesus felt toward those who carried such attitudes about children. The word is "indignant."

At our best, we should affirm these commitments with regard to the place of children in the Church of Jesus Christ:

- We believe that the Church is an intergenerational community of believers gathered for worship, witness, nurture, service, and fellowship.
- We are committed to organize the life of the Church in ways that facilitate intergenerational participation and especially the nurturing of children toward becoming committed disciples of Jesus Christ.
- We are also committed to provide age-specific and age-appropriate experiences that help the larger purposes of the kingdom of God to be taught, understood, and embraced.

Recently, as our congregation was working on some new patterns for children with regard to worship, I was challenged by the thoughts of Will Willimon in his seminal work *Pastor: The Theology and Practice of Ordained Ministry.* In his chapter on "The Pastor as Teacher," Willimon makes the following observation:

> Christian formation is the work of the whole church, not just in the classroom, but in all the activity of the church. . . . Although the purpose of Sunday worship is the glorification of God, it is also the major location for the sanctification of the faithful. Here is the major means of encountering the symbols, stories, rituals, and practices of the faith. We must take care that our Sunday service has sufficient substance to sustain our people in the rigors of discipleship. We must also ensure that the whole congregation is present when the congregation gathers—including children.[25]

These thoughts raise some serious questions for the ordering of the worship schedule in our congregations. When are the children present in the sanctuary to worship, watching their parents or other adults sing, pray, recite, give, and respond? Worship experiences that are designed especially for children have an important and needed place. If we are not careful, however, these can rob our children of a needed component in their overall Christian nurture—the need to be taught by example.

Are the children ever present when adults rise to give testimony to God's work in their lives? Are the children ever present when the offering is received and their parents rip a check out of their checkbook and place it in the offering plate? Do they come when the Eucharist is received? Do they come when the missionary is speaking? Do they ever hear the pastor preach?

Some have protested that these adult acts of worship are too far beyond the grasp of a child and that a careful congregation makes everything "kid friendly" and age specific. Says Willimon, "Children do not have to know the full meaning of these acts of corporate worship (who does?), but they ought to know the joy of full participation when the congregation gathers to enact its faith."[26]

Every congregation will have to design its own appropriate means of including children in worship. I would like to encourage you, Pastor, to make sure that the children in your congregation are included in the most important moments of worship and response that ever happen in your congregation. Let the children come.

The Pastor as Shepherd-King

THE PASTORAL ACT OF SHAPING WORLDVIEW

The last decade has brought a flurry of national events that can only be described as tragic. These life-altering episodes have now slipped into our everyday vocabulary as simple phrases that conjure up horrific images: Oklahoma City, Columbine, 9-11.

As terrible as these incidents were, we really should not be all that surprised. We've known for a long time that something is terribly wrong at the root of the human spirit. Pastors have front-row seats in the arena of human sin and its consequences. We witness the tragic result every day, and our hearts are broken.

It seems that folks are anxious to lay blame for our societal ills on some particular phenomenon or trend in the culture. "Let's put it all on Hollywood. Let's blame parents for not doing their jobs right." We can suggest that our schools aren't effective or that the glamorizing of violence in popular culture is the culprit. There is plenty of blame to go around.

The real problem is much more basic. It's worldview. When a society decides that everyone in that society gets to define for himself or herself what is right, the result is chaos. It's amazing to me that folks don't get the connection. But therein is the nature of our work. We are about the task of calling people to embrace a worldview that is distinctly Christian. We are trying to help them move their entire mindset from the kingdom of this world to the kingdom of God. Doing that requires much more than offering our folks a rather bland diet of "How to Do This" and "Ten Steps to That" and "Five Ways to Handle the Other." It requires carefully, intentionally, and prayerfully bringing them to collide with the gospel of Jesus Christ.

This is the pastoral art of shaping worldview among a congregation of people. It is long and hard work, but by grace it can be done. It requires some important things of us that are basic to our work.

For example, it requires careful and faithful proclamation of the Scriptures. The texts of the Bible are seeking to call out a community of faith that lives in this world as an authentic expression of the kingdom of God. We do a horrible disservice to the Scriptures when we approach them only to find a slick formula for addressing the felt needs of contemporary persons. We must allow the life-shaping stories and teachings of the Bible to refunction in the lives of our people, calling them to a distinctive pattern of life that is based on covenant relationship with a holy God.

We must also order the life of the church according to this Christian worldview. How do we go about structuring the program and ministry of our church? How do we make decisions about the content of each service? How do we help people in their relationships with one another experience God's very best? Do we make these decisions on current models of organizational efficiency or on the basis of what it means to live together redemptively as "aliens and strangers" in this world?

We must also be willing to be prophetic in our pastoral ministry. We are not called only to soothe the troubled minds of people with peaceful messages. We are messengers of grace to be sure, but we are also messengers of truth. Are we willing to stand before our people, who regularly find themselves enmeshed in the values of this world, and boldly call them to something different?

We have an awesome task. We have a critical task. We have the opportunity to effect real change in a chaotic world by helping to shape the worldview of its people.

PASTORAL VISITATION

A few days ago I received a letter from a friend who is a veteran pastor. He just retired from a long career of faithful and effective service to Christ's Church. One of the marks of his ministry was personal care for his people. Let me share with you a portion of his letter:

Dear Jeren: I am deeply concerned that some of our young pastors are seeing themselves more as administrators than pastors. I am aware of the need for administration and for equipping the Body to do the work of the ministry. More and more, I am seeing laypersons minister to the needs of the poor, the sick, and the needy. But at the same time, the duties of a Nazarene pastor are clearly given in the *Manual*. We are 'to care for the people by pastoral visitation, particularly the sick and the needy' (paragraph 413.5). We may have laypersons calling on them, and that is good. But the personal care of the pastor is important.

Truthfully, my way of doing pastoral care is different than that of my good friend. But his words are not lost on me. I find myself regularly overwhelmed with the demands of leading a growing church, but I am also aware that part of my core work as a pastor is to shepherd (to guide, to protect, to love, to watch over) the people. This requires being with them. So I thought about my friend's letter. I went back over what mentors taught me about being a pastor. Then I responded to the letter.

Dear Friend: I do believe that the essence of pastoral ministry is spiritual direction that necessitates being with the people. I agree that too many pastors have come to view themselves more as CEOs than as shepherds. This is, in part, a result of the pressure to be "successful" in measurable criteria. In the Church of the Nazarene, the majority of our churches are small enough (under 100 members) that "old-fashioned" pastoral care is still possible.

However, a mindset that we must avoid is that the pastor is there primarily to serve the insiders. I agree that it is important for congregations to learn the biblical truth regarding the priesthood of all believers. As you say, pastors certainly aren't the only people who can and should provide pastoral care.

In our larger churches the methods of pastoral care change of necessity. There comes a point as a church grows in size where it is physically impossible for one pastor personally to offer care to every person in the congregation. Larger churches have developed ways of dealing with this dilemma. But I wonder if many pastors in the typical Nazarene congregation have taken their cues from larger church pastors and have tried to emulate the model without having a substantive reason to do so.

Eugene Peterson writes, "Listening is in short supply in the world today; people aren't used to being listened to. I know how easy it is to avoid the tough, intense work of listening by being busy. Too much of pastoral visitation is punching the clock, assuring people we're on the job, being busy, earning our pay."[27]

Certainly the work of pastoral care today requires new strategies and methods. The methods must fit the context. Pastoral visitation in suburbia is different than it is in town and country. Technologies like E-mail, voice mail, instant messaging, and cellular phones provide new ways to regularly connect with people.

Being a pastor is about *presence*. I am Christ's representative, a sign of the presence of Jesus in the lives of people I have been called to care for. I don't want to be late for the appointment! I want to show up and be present to listen to, love, and guide these precious folks God has entrusted to me. That, in my view, is authentic pastoral visitation!

WHAT I LEARNED WHILE WAITING TO EAT BARBECUE

One of the perks of living in Kansas City is the food, especially the world-famous barbecue. Eating barbecue in this town is almost a spiritual experience to some.

Not long after moving here, I traveled about 30 minutes south of my home in order to enjoy one of my favorite barbecue haunts in Martin City. Some effort is required to enjoy this tasty treat. First of all, you have to know how to get there because the location of this restaurant is an out-of-the-way corner in an out-of-the-way village south of Kansas City. From the outside, the place looks terrible. It's an old, dark building with very few windows to let the patron know what he or she is getting into.

Then there's the challenge of parking. The small lot in front of the restaurant is always full. I parked about a quarter-mile away along the road, with half of my car hanging precariously into the drainage ditch. When I walked in, I shouldered my way through the crowd up to the hostess desk, only to discover there would be no table available for at least an hour. "No matter," I said. "I'll wait."

The waiting area would comfortably accommodate about 10 people. At least 40 of us were waiting. So 10 people sat on the benches while the rest of us stood like the occupants of an overcrowded elevator, trying hard not to invade each other's personal space too much. Finally, after 75 minutes of waiting, our names were called. We sat down, placed our orders, and when the food arrived we quickly remembered why we endured the ordeal of getting to this poorly appointed yet wonderful barbecue restaurant.

During that long waiting period, something occurred to me that changed how I look at church growth. You see, I serve a church that is in a relatively poor location with minimal visibility. Our parking lot is woefully inadequate, and the most attractive part of our facility is tucked away behind the other structures, blocked from street view. Many have been quick to tell me that if our church is ever to really experience growth, these deficits will have to be addressed. Yet in spite of our "handicaps," we have experienced pretty significant growth over the years.

Standing in the waiting area at the restaurant, getting far too familiar with people I had never met, I asked myself: *Why do these people come? Why did I come? Why would this many people endure the hassle of finding an out-of-the-way place with virtually no parking to stand scrunched together for over an hour waiting to be served?* There is only one reason. It's because they all know that once they get inside, they're going to get something that is really good.

By contrast, I've been to other restaurants that seem to have all the right stuff, but I won't be back. Not because the facility wasn't nice, but because when I got in I found nothing satisfying.

You see the point, don't you? I am not saying that external things have no impact on our churches. Location, parking, appearance of the facility—they are important matters to think about. But our primary concern must always be with what the people receive when they get in. If we are taking care to prepare solid, healthy, satisfying worship services, if people are being adequately fed, they will be back. Why? Because people are hungry. They are hungry for what is true and pure. They are hungry to experience the presence of God. If people regularly experience the power of the Spirit of God in your church, they'll put up with a lot of poor signs and cramped parking lots in order to be there.

10 TRAITS OF EFFECTIVE LEADERS

Warren Bennis is a widely recognized expert on leadership. He and a friend interviewed top executives and gifted entrepreneurs who are considered the movers and shakers of American business. From these interviews Bennis extracted some traits that seemed to be common to all effective leaders.

Self-knowledge: Effective leaders have an understanding of who they are, what their talents are, and how best to use them.

Open to feedback: Good leaders develop and value various sources of feedback on their performances. One of the best sources, says Bennis, is a spouse. Of the 40 executives of Fortune 200 companies that were studied, all but two of them were still married to their first spouse and very enthusiastic about the marriage relationship.

Eager to learn and improve: Leaders are great askers and listeners; they ask a lot of clarifying and probing questions and listen to the answers. Almost all leaders have a bias toward change, and they are very open to new information.

Curious, risk-takers: Most leaders are adventurous. They seem to walk through life with their eyebrows raised, looking for ways to challenge the status quo. They are capable of taking great risks.

Concentrate at work: There is an irresistible persistence about good leaders. They have a degree of concentration and focus that sets them apart from most people.

Learn from adversity: Almost all effective leaders have suffered significant setbacks. They used the crisis or failure in their lives to learn great lessons about people, organizations, and relationships.

Balance tradition and change: Competent leaders know better than to throw out the proverbial baby with the bath water. They are able to embrace radical change without compromising everything good about tradition. They are aware of traditions but not entrapped by them.

Open style: The best leaders operate with an open-door policy.

They are not afraid of access and feedback. They welcome criticism as an opportunity for growth.

Work well with systems: Every leader soon realizes that he or she can't handle every problem and must rely heavily on others to accomplish the necessary tasks.

Serve as model and mentors: Many leaders take great pride in those who have been trained under their supervision. They take seriously their responsibility to invest in the lives of emerging leaders so that there is always a well of leadership for the future.[28]

Being a pastor is perhaps the ultimate leadership challenge. We are required to call up a wider array of leadership skills than those in almost any other profession. These leadership qualities are applicable regardless of personality or style. Take a moment to evaluate your leadership against these ten simple observations. Are you developing as a person who can be a good leader?

SEXUAL HEALING

Roman Catholic priests gained the kind of notoriety at the turn of this century that nobody wants. When the shepherds of Christ's Church misuse their sexuality, it is particularly offensive, even to pagans. It is reasonable that those charged with the care of souls should maintain the highest levels of pure thought and appropriate action toward their people, particularly toward children.

We certainly call Nazarene pastors to the highest levels of sexual purity. This is critical not only in terms of how people are treated but also in terms of the spiritual, emotional, and physical health of the pastor. It is amazing, however, that while we demand sexual purity, we are loathe to talking much about sex. While our culture sexualizes almost everything, we who know the Author of sex remain strangely silent about how to lead our people toward sexual repentance, healing, and new patterns of behavior. Perhaps our reluctance to talk about sex has some connection to our own struggles with it.

Sex is one of the most sensitive subjects to deal with from the pulpit. It brings up many powerful emotions in our people. It may also bring up powerful emotions in the preacher. Unfortunately, the Church's response to the sexual dysfunction of our culture has been a polarity. Either we have kept silent—the head-in-the-sand approach—or we have yelled, condemned, and judged. One of the reasons that the Church has often been so ineffective in dealing with sexual issues is that we have created a culture of shame rather than a culture of truth and healing.

This is critical. People cannot deal effectively with their sexual struggles alone. Yet people will not deal honestly and openly with their sexual struggles unless and until there is created in the Church an atmosphere of grace, understanding, forgiveness, nonjudgmentalism, and healing.

This begins with leadership. In the congregation, it starts with the pastor. In the denomination, it starts with general and district leaders. I will speak here to the pastor and let other applications be made as needed and appropriate. If you have never struggled with sexual temptation, praise God! But please do not speak down to precious people in your congregation who believe that if you knew what God knows about them you would despise them. Speak as a loving father or mother whose heart is breaking for the sickness of his or her children. And if you know the personal struggle of sexual temptation, then speak as someone who is on the journey with them. You must, of course, speak appropriately and carefully, but let them know that you understand what it's like to live in a pornographic age.

Most importantly, proclaim the gospel. Sexual sin is not the unpardonable sin. It is serious, and it must be dealt with as we open our lives to the work of a holy God who desires to make us holy. So announce the good news that God is able to deliver. Give hope that the patterns of a lifetime truly can be changed. Offer the grace of Jesus, who welcomes hurting and broken people into his arms and promises never to leave them or forsake them.

Our Wesleyan message of heart holiness is a good and hopeful word to people who live in a promiscuous society. We believe and affirm that the Spirit is able and available actually to transform the hearts and minds of people. Let's put our everyday ministry where our mouths are. Let's open our mouths to speak honestly and directly with our people about the fact that sex matters and that God wants to be Ruler of our sexual thoughts, feelings, and actions. He is able to do what 1 Thessalonians 5:23 says: "[To keep] your whole spirit, soul and body . . . blameless at the coming of our Lord Jesus Christ."

NOTES

1. Kenneth D. Crow, Ph.D., "The Corps of Pastors of the Church of the Nazarene," <http://www.nazarene.org/ansr/articles/crow_96b.html>.

2. In a workshop titled, "The Unnecessary Pastor" given by Marva Dawn and Eugene Peterson. The transcript is now in book form under the same title.

3. Paragraph 413, 2001-2005 *Manual*, Church of the Nazarene.

4. Eugene Peterson lays this out eloquently in the Introduction to his wonderful book, *Working the Angles: The Shape of Pastoral Integrity* (Grand Rapids: William B. Eerdmans Publishing Co., 1987).

5. *Pulpit and Pew Research Reports, No. 3, Winter 2003.*

6. Quoted by Will Willimon in *Pastor: The Theology and Practice of Ordained Ministry*, 60.

7. Eugene H. Peterson, *A Long Obedience in the Same Direction* (Downers Grove, Ill.: Intervarsity Press, 1980), 12-13.

8. Prayer of commitment from Wesley's Covenant Service.

9. William H. Willimon, *Pastor: Theology and Practice of Ordained Ministry*, 60.

10. 1 Kings 19.

11. Patricia Pearson, "Rage!" *USA Today*, August 4, 1999.

12. Annie Dillard, *Holy the Firm*, New York: Harper Collins, 1988.

13. Henri J. M. Nouwen, *Making All Things New* (New York: Harper Collins Publishers, 1981), 24.

14. Eugene H. Peterson, *The Contemplative Pastor* (Grand Rapids: William B. Eerdmans Publishing Co., 1993), 17. (Chapter Two, *The Unbusy Pastor*, is worth the price of the book.)

15. Ibid., 23.

16. David Hansen, *The Power of Loving Your Church: Leading Through Acceptance and Grace*, Minneapolis, Bethany House Publishers, 1998, 115.

17. Quoted at <www.cybernation.com>

18. Brennan Manning, *The Wisdom of Tenderness* (New York: Harper Collins Publishers, 2002), 132.

19. Marva Dawn, *Reaching Out Without Dumbing Down* (Grand Rapids: William B. Eerdmans Publishing Co., 1995), 21

20. Professor Marva Dawn explains this in her book *A Royal Waste of Time* (Grand Rapids: William B. Eerdmans Publishing Co., 1999).

21. It is available as a 128-page, paper-bound reference book from Abingdon Press.

22. The best I have found is <http://divinity.library.vanderbilt.edu/lectionary/>

23. <http://www.growmagazine.org/research.html>

24. Some of these thoughts come from the book by William H. Willimon, *Sunday Dinner: The Lord's Supper and the Christian Life* (Nashville: Abingdon Press, 2002).

25. William H. Willimon, *Pastor: The Theology and Practice of Ordained Ministry*, 221-22.

26. Ibid., 222.

27. Eugene Peterson, *The Contemplative Pastor*, 21.

28. Adapted from chapter 12 of Warren Bennis, *Managing People Is like Herding Cats* (Provo, Utah: Executive Excellence Publishing, 1997).

ABOUT THE AUTHOR

Jeren Rowell has been senior pastor of the Church of the Nazarene in Shawnee, Kansas, for the past 13 years. Prior to his current assignment, he served in associate pastor roles for 12 years at Nampa, Idaho; Shawnee, Kansas; and Chicago. He is a graduate of Northwest Nazarene University and Olivet Nazarene University. He has also been a student at Nazarene Theological Seminary and Trinity Evangelical Divinity School.

Jeren is a frequent speaker in churches, workshops, seminary classes, retreats, and marriage enrichment events around the world. He is a writer and editor for two periodicals in the Church of the Nazarene: *The Communicator* and *Preacher's Magazine*. He is a contributor to the book *Holiness 101*. He has also contributed articles for *Holiness Today*, *Family Style*, and *Table Talk* magazines. Jeren and his wife, Starla, are certified Marriage Enrichment leaders and trainers through the Church of the Nazarene. They have four children ranging in age from 11 to 23.